D1466562

EARLIER
PHILOSOPHICAL WRITINGS

The Library of Liberal Arts
OSKAR PIEST, FOUNDER

The Library of Liberal Arts

EARLIER
PHILOSOPHICAL
WRITINGS

The Cartesian Principles

and

Thoughts on Metaphysics

BARUCH SPINOZA

Translated by

FRANK A. HAYES

Assistant Professor of Philosophy, Chatham College

with an introduction by

DAVID BIDNEY

Professor of Anthropology and Philosophy, Indiana University

· ·

The Library of Liberal Arts

published by

THE **BOBBS-MERRILL** COMPANY, INC.
A SUBSIDIARY OF HOWARD W. SAMS & CO., INC.
Publishers · INDIANAPOLIS · NEW YORK

Baruch Spinoza: 1632-1677

194.1
D454sp2

TRANSLATOR'S PREFACE

In facing the translator's traditional dilemma, I have cared primarily for accuracy, and only secondarily for style. The translation has been compared word by word with the French translation of 1954 (R. Caillois, M. Francès et R. Misrahi, *Spinoza Œuvres Complètes,* Bibliothèque de la Pléiade) and with H. H. Britan's original English translation published in 1905. I was not able to compare it with H. E. Wedeck's recent translation, which appeared after my manuscript was in the publisher's hands.

Spinoza's friends saw his manuscript through the press with great care, and since later editions were faithful to the original, there are no textual difficulties in this work. Consequently the translation may be referred to its original in any of the standard editions of Spinoza's works, such as the handsome volumes of Gebhardt or the more readily available editions of Van Vloten and Land (referred to in the notes as VL). In the translation, those footnotes which I have added are in brackets.

In Part II of the *Principles* I have not attempted to translate the term *concursus,* which Spinoza introduces in the definition of "substance." It means something like "God's sustaining causality" and is best understood through the discussion of Proposition XII in Part I. Neither have I attempted to translate the term *determinatio* introduced in Proposition XVI and explained at length in the Scholium to Proposition XXVII, although I do write it in English form as "determination." Also, throughout the second part I follow Spinoza's habit of using the verb *movere* in the passive voice: in Cartesian physics a body is always moved, because it has no force of itself whereby it could move itself. For Descartes the principal cause of motion is God (Proposition XII) and so the local motion of a body should not be confused "with the force or action that does the moving" (Definition 8).

v

In the "Thoughts on Metaphysics" I have for convenience of citation added numerals to each subsection, and in Chapter I, Part I, I have allowed myself the anachronism of translating Spinoza's *ens Rationis* by the phrase "logical being."

I am much indebted to Dr. Celestine J. Sullivan and Dr. Newton P. Stallknecht for encouraging me throughout the work of translating. I am grateful to Dr. Stuart MacClintock for scrutinizing parts of the translation in relation to the original, and for his perceptive suggestions. To Dr. David Bidney I owe a special obligation for his continuing encouragement, for his helpful criticisms, and for his courtesy in writing the Introduction. Finally, I would like to dedicate the translation to Dr. Lionel Pearson, with my thanks for his patient and good teaching.

FRANK A. HAYES

CONTENTS
. . . .

INTRODUCTION

SPINOZA'S INTERPRETATION OF DESCARTES

1. *Descartes and Spinoza on Mathematical Method*

The *Principles of the Philosophy of René Descartes* is the earliest of Spinoza's published works and the only one to bear the author's name during his lifetime. It was originally published in Latin in the fall of 1663 together with a Preface by his friend, Dr. Ludovicus Meyer, and an Appendix containing Spinoza's "Thoughts on Metaphysics." The work was translated into Dutch in 1664 by his friend Pieter Balling, a Mennonite opposed to dogmatism in religion.

Spinoza's main purpose was expository. He wished to reformulate the basic ideas of Descartes' *Principles of Philosophy* in geometric form and to synthesize the ideas contained therein with those of Descartes' other works. But as the letter to his friend and editor indicates, Spinoza did more than merely expound Descartes' thought. He tried to "prove many things in a way that is different from Descartes" and "to prove many things which Descartes merely asserts without any proof," besides adding other propositions not found in his works.[1]

In a letter to Henry Oldenburg, the secretary of the Royal Society of London, written a few days earlier in July, 1663, Spinoza explains fully the circumstances which led to the publication of his first work. We gather that he had previously dictated to Johannes Casearius, a pupil of his who lived in the same house with Spinoza in Rijnsburg, near Leiden, a summary of the second part of the *Principles* of Descartes in geometrical order together with his "Thoughts on Meta-

[1] Letter XV to Meyer, in *Correspondence of Spinoza*, tr. A. Wolf (London, 1928), p. 135. All subsequent references to Spinoza's letters are to this edition.

physics." [2] His friends in Amsterdam then asked him to prepare the first part of the *Principles* also in geometrical order, and this he completed within two weeks. He stipulated, however, that his friends should edit the Latin work for style and add a short Preface explaining that he did not accept all of Descartes' views as his own and that he had "written therein many things which are the very contrary of the views I embrace."

This Preface was written by Meyer,[3] who in it comments on the method of mathematics and explains why he regards it as the model for scientific research in philosophy and the sciences. By the method of mathematics in the universal sense, he meant the method of demonstrating conclusions from definitions, postulates, and axioms which, being clear and distinct statements and common notions of the mind, constitute the only stable foundations of human knowledge. Mathematical method, he observes, is not limited to mathematics, but may with complete assurance be applied to all the sciences and to metaphysical philosophy as well. Only in this way, as Descartes has maintained, will it be possible to establish certitude in philosophy comparable to that of mathematics.

In the "Reply to the Second Set of Objections," Descartes distinguishes in the geometrical mode of writing two things, namely, the order and the method of proof. The order consists in putting the known before the unknown and arranging deductions and proofs from intuitively known truths. The method of proof may be further subdivided into the analytic and synthetic modes, either method being compatible with mathematical order.

By the analytic method or analysis, one demonstrates "the true way by which a thing was methodically discovered and derived, as it were, effect from cause." [4] By analysis, one indi-

---

[2] Letters VIII and IX, Feb. and March, 1663, pp. 101 and 105-6.

[3] Letter XV to Meyer, Aug. 3, 1663, pp. 134-35.

[4] From *Philosophical Works of Descartes*, Vol. II, tr. F. S. Haldane and G. R. T. Ross (Cambridge University Press, 1934; republished 1955 by Dover Publications, New York 14), p. 48.

cates the process of discovery itself, how one arrived at clear and distinct ideas on a given subject, and the ground or reasons for following one order or sequence of ideas rather than another. By showing the reader the history of his ideas—how he came to accept them and the actual order of their development—the author is able to explain the source of his convictions, his fundamental assumptions, and the effects or consequences which derive from them. By demonstrating how his ideas were "made," so to speak, in his mind—their genesis and efficient cause—the author enables the reader to reconstruct his mental processes and to rediscover these truths for himself under the author's guidance. In his *Discourse* and *Meditations* this is precisely what Descartes set out to do, and this explains the highly personal method of his analysis. Should the attentive reader find himself unable to follow Descartes, he knows precisely at what point the difficulty begins and where to pursue the analysis further. The method of analysis is democratic and a priori in that it appeals only to the reader's intuitions and requires that he perform an intellectual experiment to verify the author's thought. The reader reasons a priori from known causes to their effects or consequences.

In the method of synthesis, the opposite procedure is followed. In synthesis one follows a prescribed geometric method stating a series of definitions, postulates, axioms, theorems, and problems. All conclusions are deduced from these explicitly stated premises and the reader is, so to speak, compelled to assent once he has granted the given premise or axiom. In synthesis the reader is not shown how the author discovered his premises and how he established them as absolutely certain. Instead he is given, or presented with, the data as self-evident truths which he must affirm before proceeding to the proof of the propositions or theorems. The method of synthesis is a posteriori in the sense that the given axioms, postulates, and definitions are not proved beyond reasonable doubt but are presented as if they were already established. The reader has no freedom either in the choice of the premises to which he is asked to assent or in the conclusions to be drawn from the

premises. By contrast, in analysis the reader enjoys freedom of
choice and is not compelled to give assent to either premises
or conclusions. He is given opportunity to doubt the principles
and to determine the validity of any given argument. Hence
the method of analysis may be said to be democratic and indi-
vidualistic, whereas the method of synthesis appears as authori-
tarian and impersonal.

Descartes preferred the method of analysis because it was
"the best and truest method of teaching." The reason for his
preference, he explains, is that "nothing in metaphysics causes
more trouble than the making the perception of its primary
notions clear and distinct." [5] Unlike the truths of geometry,
metaphysical truths are not in harmony with our senses and
hence cannot be comprehended unless one withdraw the mind
from all sense perceptions. One has, first of all, to establish the
indubitable truth of his metaphysical intuitions in spite of
the inclinations of the senses and customary prejudices. Hence
metaphysical method requires the use of analysis rather than
the easy assurance of synthesis as in formal geometry. The
method of analysis is akin to hypothesis in that it does not
presuppose the truth of one's axioms and definitions, but treats
them rather as truths to be established in the face of doubts
and contradictions. Of course, as Descartes soon discovered for
himself, while the method of analysis requires a maximum of
attention and meditation on the part of the reader, it is also
conducive to disagreement and criticism once the reader finds
himself unable to follow the author's mode of reasoning. In
fact, the method of analysis invites "objections and replies,"
as Descartes early recognized, whereas the method of synthesis,
by its very impersonality and rigor of form, discourages dissent.
The method of analysis may be a better method of teaching
philosophical truths to open minds, but it does not compel
assent in a hostile or closed mind as does the impersonal
method of synthesis.

Descartes did, however, concede that the method of formal
synthesis was useful in drawing attention to the distinct parts

[5] *Ibid.*, p. 49.

of each argument. Though making for greater prolixity, the method of synthesis encouraged precision and the detection of hidden assumptions. He therefore appended a series of definitions, postulates, and axioms to his "Reply to the Second Set of Objections," followed by four propositions, just to show how the method of synthesis might be utilized to supplement the method of analysis even in metaphysical philosophy. Synthesis, he argued, was no substitute for analysis in philosophy, but it was nevertheless useful as an aid in drawing attention to all the presuppositions of a given argument, some of which are bound to be overlooked in the course of analysis.

Spinoza and his friends thought likewise. They found that many who professed to be Cartesians had simply committed his doctrines to memory without any real understanding of his thought, and had merely substituted the authority of Descartes for that of Aristotle and St. Thomas. They felt there was need for a precise and concise exposition of Descartes' philosophy by the synthetic method in order that the reader might comprehend the logical order of Descartes' philosophy, even though this did not necessarily correspond to the actual order of discovery in the mind of Descartes. Meyer hoped that if a new edition of Spinoza's work were called for, it would include Spinoza's treatment of the entire third part of Descartes' *Principles,* and some further revision in the axioms.

It appears that Spinoza permitted the publication of his treatise in Dutch [6] in the hope of attracting the attention of leading political figures of the Dutch Republic, who might then permit and facilitate the publication of his other writings. What these other writings were we can only guess, but it seems reasonable to suppose that he had already completed some version of the *Short Treatise* [7] and was at work on his *Ethics,* the first part of which (or a significant portion thereof) was already being studied by the Philosophy Society of Amsterdam, organized by Simon de Vries and his friends. This serves to

6 Letter XXI to Blyenbergh, Jan. 28, 1665.

7 D. Bidney, "Joachim on Spinoza's *Tractatus De Intellectus Emendatione,*" *Philosophical Review,* January, 1942, pp. 47-65.

explain why he urged his friend Meyer to state in the Preface to the work on Descartes that the views there expounded did not necessarily coincide with his own, and in fact differed radically from his own on important issues. Spinoza admired Descartes and accepted his vision of certitude in philosophy comparable to that of mathematics, but he did not consider himself an orthodox Cartesian, and made a point of dissociating himself from Descartes.[8] The example cited by Meyer, namely, Spinoza's denial of any distinction between the will and intellect, indicates that Spinoza disagreed with Descartes' conception of the will and its relation to other modes of thought. Spinoza was, moreover, opposed to the Cartesian assertion in physics that "this or that exceeds human grasp," on the ground that this indicated only the limitations of Descartes' thought and method rather than those of the human intellect when guided by sound method.

It is important to bear in mind that both Descartes and Spinoza recognized the limitations of the geometric, synthetic method: it was a style and order of exposition which made for clarity and economy of expression, but was not a method of discovery. The geometric method provided a special apparatus for the construction of syllogisms in accord with Aristotelian logic; it did not provide any proof or demonstration of the truth of its major premises, namely, the definitions, postulates, and axioms which are accepted as given. This explains why Spinoza saw no inconsistency in expounding the views of Descartes by the geometric method and at the same time dissociating himself from some of Descartes' theses.

The trouble with the geometric method in particular lies in the fact that it compels only formal assent, just as does the syllogism once the major premises are granted, but it provides no basis for deciding which premises to affirm or deny. That is why Descartes maintained that the geometric method was not directly applicable to metaphysics, wherein the major premises must first be established after being subjected to radical doubt.

[8] Cf. Leon Roth, *Spinoza, Descartes, and Maimonides* (Oxford, 1924), pp. 44-45.

Clear and distinct ideas are not really given in metaphysics; they must rather be achieved by a process of careful, painstaking analysis which leaves no room for further doubt, as, for example, in establishing the truth of the proposition *cogito, ergo sum.*

Descartes and Spinoza distinguished, therefore, between the concept of mathematical method in general and that of geometrical method in particular. Mathematical method may be further subdivided into order and method of proof. Mathematical order refers to the order of deduction, to the arrangement of propositions whereby the known is clearly distinguished from the unknown and the latter is deduced from the former. Mathematical proof proceeds by analysis of clear and distinct ideas and seeks to establish relations between these ideas. The method is entirely a priori and makes no appeal to the data of experience.[9] Mathematical method in this general, formal sense is universal and may be applied to any subject matter whatsoever. Geometrical method, however, is a special application of mathematical method and is especially successful in dealing with lines and figures which are easily imagined and apprehended. Geometrical method or style must not be confused with mathematical method in general, since the latter is not limited to dealing with quantitative sense objects, as Gilson seems to think.[10]

The difficulty inherent in the transfer of the geometric method to philosophy may be illustrated by reference to the distinction between propositions, axioms, and postulates. In practice, as Descartes and Spinoza admitted, it is difficult to draw any sharp distinctions between them. Thus, Descartes admits in his "Reply to the Second Set of Objections" (Postulate VII) that several of his axioms might have been much better explained "and should have been brought forward as theorems if I had wished to be more exact." [11]

[9] Letter X to de Vries, about March, 1663.

[10] E. Gilson, *The Unity of Philosophical Experience* (New York, 1952), Chap. 5.

[11] *Philosophical Works of Descartes,* II, 55.

Similarly, in his Preface to Spinoza's work Meyer observes that the axioms formulated by Spinoza can be demonstrated like theorems and can more fittingly be called "propositions." Spinoza himself explains in a letter that there is no difference between a definition that explains the essence of a thing as it exists outside the understanding, and a proposition or axiom, except that an axiom is usually wider than the other two and extends to eternal truths.[12] Thus, it appears, in applying geometrical method to philosophy, both Descartes and Spinoza found it difficult to separate definitions, axioms, postulates, and propositions. A proposition that seems self-evident to one author and is treated as an axiom may be demonstrated by another. Axioms are apparently, in practice at least, simply propositions which an author considers self-evident and does not find it necessary to discuss or prove.

Both Descartes and Spinoza may be said to adhere to mathematical method in the sense that they attempt to demonstrate propositions through intellectual analysis of clear and distinct ideas and are determined to abide by the demonstrations of reason as opposed to the evidence of the senses. The senses can only determine the intellect to investigate one phenomenon rather than another, but cannot charge it with error when it perceives anything clearly and distinctly.[13] In any conflict between intellect and the senses one may doubt the evidence of the senses, but not that of reason.

2. *Spinoza as Expositor and Critic of Descartes*

While Spinoza's professed aim in writing *The Principles of the Philosophy of René Descartes* was to expound Descartes' philosophical principles in geometrical order, he could not in practice avoid introducing some criticism and ideas of his own which Descartes could hardly accept. The very attempt to arrange Descartes' ideas in geometrical order led him to change the mode of the argument, for he felt that in some instances

---

[12] Letter IX to de Vries, March, 1663.
[13] Cf. Part II, Scholium to Prop. VI, p. 69.

Descartes had failed to be convincing, and in others had ob-
scured the issue. He drew inferences from Descartes' axioms
and postulates which Descartes himself never did and would
not have done had he been aware of them. In this sense it may
be said that Spinoza read his own ideas into Descartes, and his
exposition of Descartes often tells us more about Spinoza than
about his subject. Spinoza was simply too original and creative
a writer to submerge his own thought and allow his subject to
speak for himself.

To begin with, in presenting Descartes' philosophy in geometrical order Spinoza felt it necessary to exclude all material
which could not be fitted into the scheme of definitions, axioms, and postulates which he had formulated or extracted
from Descartes. This certainly simplified the argument, but it
impoverished Descartes' thought and made him appear more
formally consistent than he really was. In addition, when
Spinoza in his "Thoughts on Metaphysics" [14] maintains that
Scripture teaches nothing repugnant to reason, he is obviously
making reason the final criterion of theological truth, and this
is a thesis which Descartes disavows. Descartes was prepared to
submit to divine authority or revelation as interpreted by the
Roman Catholic Church and was prepared to trust the Natural
Light of Reason only so long as it did not conflict with revelation.[15]

In the Prolegomenon to his treatise, Spinoza takes up the
question whether Descartes had really answered the skeptics.
Specifically, he takes up the criticism that since all things are
uncertain so long as we are ignorant of our origin, and "since
the existence of God is not known to us through itself, we apparently can never be certain of anything; and we can never
know that God exists." This is another way of saying, as has
often been said, that Descartes is involved in a vicious circle:
he first posits clarity and distinctness of ideas as the criterion
of truth (as in *cogito, ergo sum*), and then attempts to prove
the existence of God in order to guarantee the validity of clear
and distinct ideas in mathematics. We must, the critics argue,

[14] Part II, Chap. VIII, § 5.
[15] *Principles of Philosophy*, Part I, Prins. 25, 28.

either begin with the idea of God as something known per se and then infer the validity of all clear and distinct ideas from it; or else, begin with the axiom that all clear and distinct ideas are true regardless of the existence of God.

According to Spinoza's first interpretation, Descartes really maintains that we cannot doubt the clear and distinct ideas of the intellect but only the *memory* of our demonstrations and deductions. God's veracity guarantees the truth of our past demonstrations but is not needed to validate clear and distinct ideas themselves. In Spinoza's words:

> Although we do not yet know whether the author of our origin has created us to be deceived even in things which appear most evident, still we cannot, on this account, doubt things which we clearly and distinctly understand either in themselves or through a process of reasoning in which we are actually engaged. We can only doubt things which we have demonstrated heretofore, and which recur to our memory although we no longer contemplate, and have probably forgotten, the reasons for which we deduced them.

Hence God's existence can be proved through other clear and distinct ideas, even if his existence cannot be known a priori or per se.

Now in the *Principles of Philosophy* (Part I, Principle 13), Descartes does indeed refer to the fallibility of memory but also adds the possibility that the mind may have been created of such a nature that it has been deceived even in that which is most evident. Hence, he concludes, the mind can have no certain knowledge until it is acquainted with its creator. This is the antithesis of Spinoza's first interpretation, which explicitly denies that knowledge of God is necessary for the validity of clear and distinct ideas.

Spinoza apparently recognized the unsatisfactory nature of this interpretation and proceeded to provide an alternative reply.

> We grant [he writes] that besides our own existence we can be absolutely certain of nothing, however carefully we attend to its demonstration, so long as we have no clear and dis-

tinct concept of God which enables us to affirm that God is absolutely truthful, just as the idea we have of a triangle compels us to conclude that its three angles are equal to two right angles.

This does not mean, however, that we must first prove the existence of God before we can affirm the truth of clear and distinct ideas. All that is necessary is that we have a clear and distinct idea of God regardless of whether he actually exists or not.

We can be certain of nothing, not indeed while we are ignorant of God's existence (for we have not spoken of this matter), but while we have no clear and distinct idea of him.

Spinoza, it appears, here separates the clear and distinct idea of God from the proof of the existence of God and argues merely that a clear and distinct idea of God is necessary for the validity of mathematical truths.

Spinoza's argument may be summed up as follows: Let us begin with a clear and distinct idea of God and a clear and distinct idea of a triangle. We cannot be certain of the truth or validity of our idea of a triangle so long as we entertain the possibility that God or the author of our nature may deceive us. If, however, we have a clear and distinct idea of God, it follows that God, or the absolutely perfect being, cannot be a deceiver. Thus, a clear and distinct idea of God leads to knowledge of the veracity of God. The idea of the veracity of God will lead us to infer the veracity of the human mind in conceiving clear and distinct ideas; that is, from the veracity of God we infer the veracity of clear and distinct ideas. Thus, we have no need to prove the existence of God in order to prove the validity of clear and distinct ideas. We begin with clear and distinct ideas of God and things, and from the veracity of God alone infer the veracity of the mind and the truth of clear and distinct ideas. Later we can demonstrate the necessary existence of God from our clear and distinct idea of him. Ultimately, we begin with the *fact* of clear and distinct ideas of God and of things, and *infer*, first, the veracity of God, and second, the veracity of the mind and its clear and distinct ideas. Clear and distinct ideas are *given;* their truth must be *inferred* either directly (as in the case of God) or indirectly (as in the case of the human mind).

The pivot of Spinoza's argument turns on this: we separate and distinguish the *fact* of the clarity and distinctness of our ideas from the question of their *truth* and validity. "We have," he remarks, "a clear and distinct idea of a triangle, although we do not know whether the author of our nature deceives us." So long as we lack a clear and distinct idea of God or of a triangle we may continue to doubt many things concerning them, but once we have a clear and distinct idea the mind is compelled to affirm certain properties of these objects. Unless, however, we begin with the idea of God, the author of our nature, we cannot be absolutely certain of the truth of our inferences besides the *cogito.* Hence we must begin with the clear and distinct idea of God and from it infer the veracity of God and the veracity of the human mind in conceiving clear and distinct ideas. In all instances we infer veracity from clear and distinct ideas, not clear and distinct ideas from the veracity of God.

Thus we find Spinoza presenting us with two alternative replies to Descartes' critics. In the first reply he maintains the autonomy and intrinsic validity of clear and distinct ideas comparable to the idea of the *cogito.* Here the idea of God is introduced only to guarantee the continuity of memory in demonstration, not the validity of direct intuition. In the second reply the idea of God's veracity is essential for establishing the truth of clear and distinct ideas, but the proof of his existence is not required for establishing their validity. Spinoza's arguments are indeed instructive and throw much light on a highly controversial subject. As Gilson has observed,[16] modern students of Descartes might well have profited by taking into consideration Spinoza's suggestive interpretation of him.

The problem remains, however, whether Spinoza's interpre-

[16] E. Gilson, "Spinoza Interprète de Descartes," *Chronicon Spinozanum,* III (1923), 68-87.

tation and replies on behalf of Descartes are in accord with the historical Descartes. Descartes himself did not separate the question of the clarity and distinctness of ideas from that of their objective truth, as Spinoza would have him do. The example of the *cogito* led Descartes to identify clear and distinct ideas with true ones. Hence he attempted to prove the existence of God prior to the veracity of God, whereas Spinoza infers the veracity from the idea of God and leaves the question of God's existence in abeyance as irrelevant to the immediate argument. It is to be noted, however, that in his formal exposition of Descartes in the text, Spinoza does follow him in first proving the existence of God (Propositions V, VI, VII) and then demonstrating that God does not deceive (Proposition XIII) before finally concluding that whatever we clearly and distinctly perceive is true (Proposition XIV). This, as is evident, is not in accord with the argument of the Prolegomenon.

Spinoza's interpretation does indicate how Descartes *might have* avoided the dilemma in which he became involved: by affirming unequivocally either the autonomy and intrinsic validity of clear and distinct ideas independent of God, or the primacy of the idea of God as the source of all truth in clear and distinct ideas. The historical Descartes tends to waver now and then, his mathematical studies leading him to affirm the intrinsic worth and truth of clear and distinct ideas (with God simply validating the memory of past intuitions) and his metaphysical doubt leading him to deny the validity of such ideas unless supported by proof of the existence and veracity of God.

Historically, the distinction here introduced between the fact of clear and distinct ideas and their objective truth is an important one for an understanding of Spinoza's *Ethics*. It serves to explain why Spinoza began his *Ethics* with clear and distinct ideas of substance and attribute before undertaking to prove the actual existence of an absolutely perfect substance whom he called God. His study of Descartes also convinced him that since God was the source of all truth in human thought, it was necessary to begin with the idea of God through

whom all things exist and are conceived, rather than begin
with things as the Scholastics did, or with ideas of things as
Descartes tried to do.[17]

In his geometrical exposition of Descartes' thought, Spinoza
began by simply taking over, with slight modifications, the ten
definitions to be found in the appendix to the "Reply to the
Second Set of Objections." Here it is of special interest to note
that Spinoza made no attempt to resolve the differences between the two definitions of substance to be found in Descartes'
Principles of Philosophy (I, 51) and in the "Reply." He merely
restates the earlier definition from the "Reply," which reads:

> Everything in which anything is immediately contained, as
> in a subject, or through which anything we perceive exists—
> that is, any property, or quality, or attribute of which we
> have in ourselves a real idea—is called *substance*.

Here substance is the subject of properties or attributes and
Descartes distinguished mind or mental substance and body or
extended substance (Definitions 6 and 7). There are only these
two kinds of substance, but there can be as many particular
substances as there are minds or bodies—as there are subjects.
Spinoza ignores the definition of Descartes' *Principles*, which
reads:

> By substance, we can understand nothing else than a thing
> which so exists that it needs no other thing in order to exist.
> And in fact only one single substance can be understood
> which clearly needs nothing else, namely, God. . . . That is
> why the word substance does not pertain *univoce* to God
> and to other things, as they say in the Schools, that is, no
> common signification for this appellation which will apply
> equally to God and to them can be distinctly understood.[18]

According to this second definition, substance is unique and
is a term applied correctly only to God. Descartes, however,

[17] See remarks attributed by Tschirnhaus to Spinoza, quoted in Gilson,
ibid., p. 87.

[18] From *Philosophical Works of Descartes*, Vol. I, tr. F. S. Haldane and
G. R. T. Ross (Cambridge University Press, 1934; republished 1955 by
Dover Publications, New York 14), pp. 239-40.

continues to apply the term to "created substances" such as mind and body.

When we turn to Spinoza's *Ethics*, however, we find a definition of substance which is strongly reminiscent of Descartes' later definition. Definition Three of the *Ethics* reads:

> By substance, I understand that which is in itself and is conceived through itself; in other words, that, the conception of which does not need the conception of another thing from which it must be formed.[19]

Spinoza's definition really combines both of Descartes' definitions of substance. Substance is in itself, as in a subject of attributes, and it is conceived through itself alone, so that it needs no other thing to be or be conceived. Spinoza was more consistent than Descartes in recognizing no "created substances" and in reducing mind and body to the status of modes. This is but another illustration of the fact that Spinoza concealed his own views at the time he was expounding Descartes and deliberately refrained from including material to be found in the works of Descartes which would have unnecessarily complicated his presentation in geometrical form.

In the examples of the geometrical mode of argument appended to the "Reply to the Second Set of Objections," [20] Descartes devotes the first three propositions to proofs of the existence of God. Proposition I states that "the knowledge of the existence of God proceeds from the mere consideration of His nature." This is the well-known ontological argument that necessary existence is contained in the concept of God or the supremely perfect being. Proposition II gives an "a posteriori demonstration of God's existence from the mere fact that the idea of God exists in us." This proof is a mode of the causal argument. The idea of God and the objective reality of this idea is contained in us neither formally nor eminently and must, therefore, have God as its cause. In Proposition III, "the existence of God is proved by the fact that we, who pos-

---

19 *Ethics*, ed. James Gutmann (New York, 1949), p. 41.
20 *Philosophical Works of Descartes*, II, 57-58.

sess this idea, ourselves exist." Here the argument runs as follows: I have not the power of conserving myself, else I should not lack any perfections or attributes. Since I cannot exist without being conserved, some other being must conserve me. This being who conserves me has the power of self-conservation and hence cannot lack any perfection. This being must be absolutely perfect, that is to say, God.

In his geometrical exposition, Spinoza accepts without criticism the first two propositions or proofs (in Propositions V and VI) but rejects as unsatisfactory Descartes' third proof. It is of interest to examine Spinoza's criticism and his substitute proof of Descartes' third proposition.

Descartes based his third proof of the existence of God on two axioms, Eight and Nine. Axiom Eight states: "That which can effect what is greater [*majus*] or more difficult [*difficilius*] can also accomplish what is less [*minus*]." Axiom Nine states that "it is a greater thing to create or conserve substance than the attributes or properties of substance; it is not, moreover, a greater thing to create than to conserve its existence." Spinoza finds both of these axioms unintelligible and therefore does not list them among the ten axioms which he derives from Descartes. He professes to have difficulty in understanding the terms "difficult" and "easier"; they are, he says, relative terms which vary with the cause and lack any absolute meaning. A spider, he points out, easily weaves a web which men would weave only with the greatest difficulty.

Yet Spinoza does accept Descartes' Axiom Seven, which he restates (Axiom 5) to read: "If a thinking thing knows of any perfections which it lacks, it will at once give them to itself if they are in its power." According to Descartes, the will tends infallibly toward the good that it clearly knows; and the will knows that it is a greater good to possess perfections that it lacks than not to possess them. Hence it will immediately give these perfections to itself if they are in its power. For Descartes, *a greater good and a greater perfection are identical.* Hence Axiom Eight of Descartes can be interpreted to say:

That which can effect a greater good or perfection can also accomplish a lesser good or perfection, since the lesser good is easier for it to obtain. The greater perfection presupposes the lesser perfection. "Easier" and "more difficult" may be understood in this context as requiring more or less effort to acquire a given degree of perfection.

In his own exposition Spinoza wrestles with Descartes' Axiom Eight and can find no acceptable meaning. As mentioned above, he first points out that the terms "easy" and "difficult" have no absolute meaning, but only a relative meaning. Descartes could accept this. The only point at issue is, relative to what? If we take it to mean relative to ego's nature or perfection (since we know only the *cogito*), then the axiom will state: An ego which can accomplish a greater perfection can also accomplish a less.

Spinoza complicates the issue unnecessarily by suggesting a variety of meanings of the terms "easily" and "laboriously." First, he suggests that by "laboriously" Descartes could not mean the impossible, and by "easily" he could not mean that which implies no contradiction or the possible. There is no mean, he points out, between the possible and the impossible, just as there is no mean between something and nothing. Hence he denies that he who can do the impossible can also do the possible. This, Descartes might reply, is a straw argument, since he nowhere identifies the difficult with the impossible. Secondly, Spinoza suggests that by "greater" and "more difficult" Descartes means that which is more perfect, and by "more easily" that which is less perfect. This Spinoza pretends to find obscure because he denies that he who can do more can at the same time and in the same work do less; for example, if I use my powers in conserving my being, I cannot devote them to accomplishing lesser things, even though easier. This, it seems, is to give the terms "easily" and "difficult" a very special meaning not intended by Descartes at all. Descartes did not mean that he who achieves one perfection can simultaneously and in the same work achieve a lesser or easier perfection. If one is employing all his efforts and attention on a given task, he obviously cannot at the same time do a lesser one, no matter how easy, just as an individual who has spent all his money to purchase a given object has no money left to buy anything else, no matter how little it costs. All Descartes meant is the perfectly simple notion that he who is capable of a greater perfection is also capable of a lesser one, since the greater perfection involves more power and reality than the lesser. This is in agreement with the axiom (Axiom 8 in Spinoza, 4 in Descartes) that whatever reality or perfection there is in a thing exists either formally or eminently in its first and adequate cause. An eminent cause, in other words, contains greater perfection than its effect and produces this effect more easily than a formal cause. The example of the spider spinning its web is misleading, since it compares different species of animals in terms of their organic equipment. Man is said to be more perfect than the spider because he contains more perfection or reality than the spider but not because he can perform all skills as well as, or better than, a spider.

As regards Descartes' Axiom Nine, which states in part that "it is a greater thing to create or conserve substance than the attributes or properties of substance," Spinoza denies that it is true at all. His argument is that attribute and substance do not differ formally or essentially but differ only in thought. This criticism merely indicates that Descartes and Spinoza do not define attribute in the same way. For Spinoza, substance and attribute do not differ formally. As may be seen from the *Ethics* and from his correspondence,[21] Spinoza claims that substance and attribute are identical and differ only in that attribute is substance from the perspective of the intellect, just as "plane" and "white" are identical and differ only in relation to a given perceiver. Obviously, according to this definition it is not a greater thing to create or conserve substance than its attributes.

Descartes, however, does not distinguish clearly and dis-

[21] Letter IX to de Vries, March, 1663.

tinctly between modes, qualities, properties, and attributes. As he explains in his *Principles* (I, 56):

> And, indeed, when we here speak of modes we mean nothing more than what elsewhere is termed *attribute* or *quality*. But when we consider substance as modified or diversified by them, I avail myself of the word *mode;* . . . and finally when we more generally consider that these modes or qualities are in substance we term them *attributes*. And because in God any variableness is incomprehensible, we cannot ascribe to Him modes or qualities; but simply attributes. And even in created things that which never exists in them in any diverse way, like existence and duration in the existing and enduring thing, should be called not qualities or modes, but attributes.[22]

Descartes then proceeds to distinguish attributes which pertain to things and those which pertain to thought (I, 57). Time, for example, is said to differ from duration in that the former is only a mode of thought. Later on (I, 61), Descartes differentiates mode from substance by observing that "we can clearly conceive substance without the mode which we say differs from it, while we cannot reciprocally have a perception of this mode without perceiving the substance."[23] By contrast, there is a "distinction of reason" between substance and any one of its attributes (I, 62). For example, duration is distinct from substance only by thought. Similarly extension and thought differ from their corresponding substances only in thought (I, 63).

If attribute and substance differ only in thought, then it does become difficult to maintain that "it is a greater thing to create or conserve substance than the attributes or properties of substance." To make sense, we must assume that at the time Descartes wrote the *Meditations* and the appendix to the "Reply to the Second Set of Objections" he employed the term "attribute" loosely to refer to any quality or property. He intended to differentiate substance, the subject of qualities or attributes, from the qualities or attributes which exist in and

[22] *Philosophical Works of Descartes*, I, 241-42.
[23] *Ibid.*, I, 244.

through it. Hence substance is logically prior to its "attribute" and can be conceived without it. An attribute presupposes a subject or substance through which it exists and is perceived. As employed here, Descartes means by attribute what Spinoza means by mode (*Ethics,* I, Definition 5). Since there is more reality or perfection to substance than to mode it is a greater thing to create or conserve substance than mode. This usage of "mode" accords, as we have noted, with Descartes' own distinction between substance and mode in the *Principles* (I, 61). Spinoza, however, employed "attribute" in the sense in which Descartes employed it later in the *Principles,* namely, as constituting the essence of a given substance, and from this perspective, as Descartes himself realized, substance and attribute differ only in thought but not in reality. In the light of the *Principles* only, Axiom Nine does not make sense.

We turn now to examine Spinoza's own proof of Proposition VII (Part I; Descartes' Proposition III), which states that "the existence of God is also demonstrated from the fact that we ourselves, who have the idea of him, exist." Spinoza's argument runs as follows: since (by Axiom 6, Descartes' Axiom 10) either possible or necessary existence is contained in the idea or concept of every thing, the greater the degree of perfection of a thing, the greater is the necessity of its existence; "and, conversely, in proportion as a thing entails by its own nature necessary existence, the more perfect it is" (*quo magis necessarium existentiam res sua natura involvit, eo perfectior est*), (Lemma 1). In brief, existence and perfection are inseparable and vary proportionately—the greater the perfection, the greater the necessity of existence. This proposition presupposes that there are degrees of existence from the impossible through the possible to the absolutely necessary, corresponding to the degrees of perfection from zero through the finite to the infinite. "Hence it follows that whatever entails necessary existence is entirely perfect being, or God" (Corollary). Next, Lemma Two states that "the nature of a being which has the power to conserve itself entails necessary existence." This follows from Spinoza's Axiom Ten (Descartes' Axiom 2), which states that the power to conserve is the same as the power to create. A thing which has the power to create itself and to conserve itself has necessary existence because it depends on no external cause. From this it may be demonstrated (Proposition VII) that since I exist and yet lack the power to conserve myself, therefore I must be conserved by a being or power who exists necessarily and who is therefore absolutely perfect. That is to say, from the fact of *ego sum,* it follows that God necessarily exists.

Spinoza's own proof of God's existence is indeed much more complicated than Descartes' original proof. He has to assume as axiomatic that existence and perfection are inseparable and vary proportionately. He also supposes, as Descartes does not, that degrees of perfection from zero through the finite to the infinite correspond to degrees of existence from the impossible through the possible to the absolutely necessary. This is a highly questionable assumption on which Spinoza leans heavily, but which he himself attacked earlier (when he attributed it to Descartes), denying that there was a mean between the possible and the impossible. By contrast, while Descartes states in Axiom Ten that possible or contingent existence is contained in the concept of a finite thing, and necessary existence in the concept of a supremely perfect being, he nowhere speaks of degrees of necessary existence. For Descartes there is no mean between the impossible and possible existence, or between possible and necessary existence. There is a leap from the realm of possible existence to necessary existence as there is from the finite to the infinite. In Spinoza, by contrast, it is assumed that there are degrees of existence corresponding to degrees of perfection, and hence that the more perfect exists more necessarily (*magis necessariam existentiam*) than does the less perfect. For Descartes there are degrees of perfection and reality, but these do not correspond to degrees of existence. Only in the case of the absolutely perfect Being is necessity of existence converted into an essential attribute. All other forms of perfection have only possible or contingent existence, since they depend for their essence and existence on the will and power of God.

It is possible to restate Descartes' third proof of the existence of God without employing his disputed Axioms Eight and Nine, and without making Spinoza's questionable assumptions, somewhat as follows: (1) I lack the power of conserving myself from moment to moment since it does not follow from the clear and distinct idea of my nature as a thinking being; (2) hence, some being who has the power of self-conservation conserves me; (3) this being who has the power of self-conservation also has the attributes of absolute perfection and necessary existence, and hence is God; (4) thus the fact of my existence is proof of the existence of God.

Spinoza's own demonstration of this proposition is, basically, dependent on similar arguments: (1) The nature of a being who has power of self-conservation involves necessary existence and absolute perfection (Lemma 2; Axiom 10); (2) I exist but lack power of self-conservation; (3) I am conserved by an absolutely perfect being who exists necessarily, that is to say, God. Spinoza's Lemma One, with its supposition of degrees of perfection and corresponding degrees of existence, is not at all necessary to his proof of Proposition VII.

It is a matter of historical interest to note here that Spinoza incorporated the basic argument of Lemma One and Proposition VII in his second alternative proof for the existence of God in his *Ethics*.[24] There he first states as an axiomatic truth that—

inability to exist is impotence, and, on the other hand, ability to exist is power, as is self-evident. . . . But we ourselves exist, either in ourselves or in something else which necessarily exists. Therefore the Being absolutely infinite, that is to say, God, necessarily exists.

While Spinoza affirms axiomatically that ability to exist is power, this is self-evident only if we assume Lemma One of his *Principles of the Philosophy of René Descartes;* Spinoza

[24] *Ethics*, I, Prop. XI.

does not give it in his list of axioms at the beginning of the *Ethics*. This is but another illustration of how Spinoza employed an argument in his own work which he had previously claimed to have derived from Descartes.

SPINOZA'S "THOUGHTS ON METAPHYSICS"

Spinoza's "Thoughts on Metaphysics," which is appended to his geometrical exposition of Descartes, is composed of two parts and is written in the analytical manner of the *Principles of Philosophy*. Part One discusses basic metaphysical concepts such as the definition of being and the modes of thought and being, essence and existence. Here emerges for the first time Spinoza's conception of such terms as the necessary, the impossible, the possible, and the contingent—ideas which are basic to an understanding of his *Ethics*. In addition, the important distinction is first clearly drawn between the concept of eternity, which pertains to God or uncreated substance, and duration or time, which is a mode of thought applied to the existence of finite, created things. There is also a simple and clear presentation of the meaning of the true and the false, and the relativity of good and evil, which is valuable for an understanding of his later work. Throughout Part One there is constant reference to the idea of God and how the various terms discussed may be understood when applied to him.

Part Two is primarily concerned with a discussion of the attributes of God. Spinoza, like Descartes, gives a special place to the attribute of thought, which is said to pertain to God as the infinite, uncreated substance, and excludes the attribute of extension, which pertains to bodies alone. The other attributes discussed are those logical distinctions which are essential and peculiar to God. Some of the attributes of God, such as intelligence, will, life, omnipotence, and the like, explain his active essence. Others, such as unity, eternity, necessity, and the like, describe his mode of existing (Chapter XI). While Spinoza's division of the attributes is original, the general approach is reminiscent of Descartes, Maimonides and Thomas Aquinas.

This point is further demonstrated by his assertion that will, intellect, and power are not separated and distinct in God (Chapter VIII). Since no object of God's knowledge exists outside God, he is himself the object of his knowledge (Chapter VII). This thesis is reminiscent of Descartes' position, which denies any eternal truths or ideas independent of God and affirms that all truths depend on the infinite will and intellect of God. Historically this thesis may be traced back to the Aristotelian doctrine that "active intellect" alone may be attributed to God and not "potential intellect." [25]

The subject which merits special consideration is Spinoza's treatment of the concept of free will in God and man. Through Meyer's Preface Spinoza had made a special point of indicating that he did not find himself in accord with Descartes' views on will, especially with the latter's distinction of the will and the intellect.

In his *Principles of Philosophy* (I, 32) Descartes states:

> that in us there are but two modes of thought, the perception of the understanding and the action of the will. . . . Thus sense-perception, imagining, and conceiving things that are purely intelligible, are just different methods of perceiving; but desiring, holding in aversion, affirming, denying, doubting, all these are the different modes of willing.[26]

The faculty of understanding is essentially passive; the faculty of willing is essentially active. The disparity of will and intellect is said to be a major source of error inasmuch as will assents to confused and false ideas as well as to clear and distinct ones. The mind's freedom is demonstrated in doubting, in its self-determination to keep assent and denial within the limits set by the intellect insofar as it conceives clear and distinct ideas. Error is the result of our abuse of our free will in giving consent prematurely. As Spinoza puts it, "for man error is nothing but the privation of a perfect and right use of freedom" (Scholium to Proposition XV, Part I).

---

[25] Cf. Maimonides, *Guide for the Perplexed*, Part II, Chap. XVIII.
[26] *Philosophical Works of Descartes*, I, 232.

Historically speaking, the Cartesian definition of will may be said to combine the Stoic notion of will as a faculty of choice with reference to good and evil objects. This appears most clearly in the *Meditations,* where Descartes states that our free will—

> consists only in the fact that we can make a choice; we can do a given thing or not do it—that is to say, we can affirm or deny, pursue or avoid. Or more properly, our free will consists only in the fact that in affirming or denying, pursuing or avoiding the things suggested by the understanding, we behave in such a way that we do not feel that any external force has constrained us in our decision.[27]

Here will is identified with power of choice with reference to truth and falsity of ideas as well as to objects of desire and aversion. In other words, the will has a theoretical as well as a practical function. It forms judgments of the truth and falsity of ideas, affirming and denying whether ideas conform to existing things; and it also chooses the acts the individual is inclined to perform. Descartes does not differentiate between the will as a faculty of judgment and the will as a faculty of choice, but combines both functions under "power of choosing."

In his "Thoughts on Metaphysics" Spinoza intentionally breaks with the Cartesian definition of will, though he continues to maintain the doctrine of free will. "Will," he states, "is the affirmation or denial that a thing is good" (Part II, Chapter XII, § 11). Will is now identified with the mind's essential function of affirmation and denial, that is, of judgment. From this it follows that the human will is free to the extent that the human mind is self-determined to doubt and to make affirmations and denials. In Spinoza's terms, "those mental actions [affirmations and denials] . . . which have no other cause than human mind are called 'volitions.' Now, when the human mind is regarded as the sufficient cause of such actions it is called 'will'" (Part II, Chapter XII, § 8). Spinoza is in complete agreement with Descartes that the human will is intrinsically

---

[27] Descartes, *Meditations,* tr. Laurence J. Lafleur, "Library of Liberal Arts" series, No. 29 (New York, 1960), p. 55.

free; he differs from the latter in identifying will with the act
of judgment. Furthermore, will, for Spinoza, is not indifferent
or indeterminate, because mind by nature is not indifferent in
thinking or judging. The mind is essentially active and free
in affirming and denying its thoughts and hence an indifferent
will is really a contradiction in terms. For the will to be indifferent it would have to be "stripped of thought" and therefore cease to exist. Mind or a thinking thing acts and expresses
itself through determinate acts of will; only a creature that
lacks mind, like Buridan's ass,[28] would remain indifferent, or
in a state of indecision, indefinitely. The judgment or decision
not to make a particular choice in a given situation, as in the
case of doubt, is itself an act of free will. Will and choice, according to Spinoza, are not to be confused.

Finally, will and appetite are distinct from one another.
Will judges whether objects of appetite are good or evil and
hence whether given objects are to be pursued or shunned.
The appetite originates independently of will but in an intelligent being depends upon will for its satisfaction. That is why
Spinoza explicitly rejects the notion derived from Thomas
Aquinas and ultimately from Aristotle that will is *appetitus
sub ratione boni*,[29] because to do so would be to grant that
free will consists of freedom of choice. For Spinoza, the essence
of will is the act of judgment and not the choice which results
from the judgment of good and evil. One may be indifferent
in choosing but not in willing to choose or not to choose.
Freedom of will is inescapable. The problem is not to prove
whether the will is free, but rather, whether it can be said not
to be free. It is significant to note that Descartes himself admitted the possibility of the freedom of indifference but rele-
gated it to "the lowest grade of liberty" ("Meditation IV").
For Descartes, freedom of indifference was possible because he
identified freedom of will, in part, with freedom of choice, and
ultimately with freedom of appetite. For Spinoza, as mentioned

28 See p. 157, n.
29 Frederick Copleston, S.J., *A History of Philosophy* (Westminster,
Maryland, 1962), II, 380-81.

above, freedom of will pertains only to judgment; will and appetite and choice are distinct from one another.[30]

The problem that apparently bothered Spinoza most, and to which he returned again and again, was how to reconcile divine omnipotence and omniscience with human freedom. Descartes had faced this problem in his *Principles of Philosophy* and had concluded piously that our finite thought cannot grasp the infinite mind of God and that we simply do not know how God leaves man freedom of choice. In his "Thoughts on Metaphysics" Spinoza reiterates this profession of ignorance in his own name (Part I, Chapter III). We see clearly and distinctly, he argues, that we are free in our actions, and at the same time perceive with equal clarity that everything depends on God and that nothing exists except what has been decreed by God from eternity. Both propositions must be true, even though they appear to be logically incompatible. Yet, "to reconcile our freedom of choice with God's predestination exceeds human grasp." Later in his *Ethics,* Spinoza resolved the problem by denying human freedom of will in favor of divine omnipotence.

In conclusion, it may be said that Spinoza's *Principles of the Philosophy of René Descartes* together with his "Thoughts on Metaphysics" are historically significant not only for an understanding of what Descartes meant to Spinoza but also for an appreciation of the development of Spinoza's thought. The geometrical mode of demonstration made it necessary for him to exclude a great deal of material and to select and abstract only those axioms, definitions and propositions which could be fitted together into a coherent whole. This, as noted, oversimplified the exposition and made Descartes far more formally consistent than he actually was. At times, as in his exposition of Descartes' third proof of the existence of God (Part I, Proposition VII), Spinoza attempted to improve on Descartes by introducing arguments of his own which Descartes would

[30] David Bidney, *The Psychology and Ethics of Spinoza* (New York, 1962), pp. 115-28.

surely have rejected. Even when not critical of Descartes, Spinoza read his own ideas into the former's work; the more he tried to submerge his own thought and speak for Descartes, the more he succeeded in speaking only for himself. He repeatedly confused his own ideas with those of Descartes in a manner which would have led Descartes to plead that what he needed most was protection from his friends and disciples.

Spinoza derived much profit from apprenticing himself to Descartes and always spoke of him with great esteem and respect. By far the most important lessons he learned from Descartes were faith in reason and distrust of dogmas and established traditions in philosophy. He followed Descartes' example in attempting to apply a universal, mathematical method for the demonstration of truth in metaphysics and the sciences. He agreed with Descartes that rational, intuitive knowledge of the existence and nature of God constituted the first principle of metaphysical and scientific knowledge and provided the ultimate answer to radical skepticism. Notwithstanding some significant differences from Descartes, especially as regards the latter's distinction between natural and supernatural truth, Spinoza shared with Descartes the vision of the unity of human knowledge and the harmony, in principle, of science, philosophy and religion.

DAVID BIDNEY

EARLIER PHILOSOPHICAL

WRITINGS

LOUIS MEYER'S PREFACE TO THE WORTHY READER

It is the unanimous opinion of everyone interested in more than a common knowledge of things that the method of the mathematicians in investigating and propounding scientific matters by demonstrating conclusions from definitions, postulates, and axioms is the best and surest means of searching out and teaching the truth. And rightly so. For certain and assured knowledge of a thing that is yet unknown can be drawn or derived only from things already known with certainty, and so things known with certainty must necessarily be selected and arranged beforehand as, so to speak, a stable foundation upon which the whole edifice of human knowledge may afterward be superimposed without fear of its suddenly sinking or falling in ruins at the slightest touch. That the notions which students of mathematics classify as definitions, postulates, and axioms are just such foundations of knowledge, no one who has so much as saluted that noble discipline from the threshold can possibly doubt. Definitions are simply the clearest possible explanations of the terms and words by which the matters to be discussed are designated. Postulates and axioms—or the common conceptions of the mind—are such clear and perspicuous statements that no one who has merely understood the words aright can in any way refuse to assent to them.

Although this is so, yet one will find that apart from mathematics the sciences rarely follow this method; instead the whole business is accomplished by a different method, worlds apart from this, in which definitions and divisions are interwoven and occasionally interspersed with questions and explanations. For almost everyone used to think, and even now many who have put their minds to the acquisition and formulation of the sciences still think, that the first method is peculiar to mathematical studies and that the other sciences should despise and reject it. So it has come about that authors do not prove with demonstrative arguments what they put before the public, but only heap up verisimilitudes and probable arguments, bringing to light in this way a hodgepodge of huge books in which you will find nothing stable and certain; indeed, all are full of contention and disagreement, and what is proved by one with a few trifling reasons is at once confuted by another, and demolished and scattered by the same weapons; so that a mind yearning for unshakable truth, thinking to enter upon the quiet waters of study and to cross with a safe and prosperous passage in order to gain at length the long desired harbor of knowledge, instead sees itself tossing about in a fierce sea of opinions, surrounded everywhere by storms of contention, and incessantly thrown and dragged about by waves of uncertainty, with no hope of ever emerging.

Yet there have been some who thought otherwise and, pitying the miserable condition of philosophy, have left this common and trite way of handling the sciences to enter upon a new one, though it was arduous and bristling with difficulties, so that they might leave to posterity the parts of philosophy other than mathematics demonstrated with method and mathematical certainty. Some reduced to this order the philosophy customarily taught in the schools, while others offered to the world of letters a new philosophy, discovered through their own labors. Although this labor had been undertaken by many over a long period with indifferent success, there at last arose that splendid light of our age, René Descartes, who, after he had by his new method dragged from the shadows into the light whatever in mathematics had been inaccessible to the ancients, and whatever else his contemporaries could desire, then laid down the unshakable foundations of philosophy upon which many truths can be erected with mathematical order and certainty, as he himself demonstrated, and as is more apparent than the light of day to everyone who has carefully studied his never to be sufficiently praised writings.

Although the philosophical writings of this noble and incomparable man follow a mathematical system and order of demonstration, still they are not worked out by the method habitually used in the *Elements* of Euclid and in other geometries, where propositions and their demonstrations follow upon and are related to definitions, postulates, and axioms set out at the beginning; instead, he follows an entirely different way which he calls the true and best way of teaching—the analytic. For near the end of the "Reply to the Second Set of Objections," he recognizes two ways of demonstrating with certainty: one by analysis, "which shows the precise way in which a thing has been methodically discovered, even, as it were, a priori"; the other by synthesis, "which uses a long series of definitions, assumptions, axioms, theorems, and questions, so that if anything in the consequences is denied, it is at once shown to be contained in the premises, and so extorts the assent of the most contrary and obstinate reader."

However, although certainty beyond all hazard of doubt may be found in both ways of demonstration, the two ways are not equally useful and convenient to everyone. For most people, who are inexperienced in the mathematical sciences and are consequently ignorant of the method by which they are propounded (synthesis) and by which they are discovered (analysis), are unable to follow the matters handled and demonstrated with certainty in these books, and cannot explain them to others. So it has come about that many, either gripped by blind passion or led by the authority of others, have assumed the name Cartesian, but have only committed his opinions and doctrines to memory. When speech falls from their mouths, they prate and babble at length, but do not know how to demonstrate anything, just as the addicts of the Peripatetic philosophy used to do and still do to this day. To help such people I have time and again hoped that some-one skilled in both analytic and synthetic order, versed in the writings of Descartes, and deeply knowledgeable in his philosophy, would agree to reduce to synthetic order what Descartes had written in the analytic, and to demonstrate it in the familiar geometrical manner. Indeed, although abundantly conscious of my slender talents and quite unequal to so great a work, I often intended to do it myself, and even made a beginning, but other affairs by which I am often distracted prevented my finishing it.

So I was most happy to learn from our author that he had dictated to one of his pupils, while teaching him the Cartesian philosophy, the second part of the *Principles* entire and a fragment of the third, demonstrated in the geometrical manner, together with some important and rather difficult questions aired in metaphysics and yet not resolved by Descartes; and that at the persistent pleading and insistence of his friends had agreed that these writings, corrected and enlarged by himself, should be published in one volume. Whereupon I too expressed my pleasure at this, and at the same time freely offered my help, if he should need it in the editing. Furthermore, I persuaded and even demanded that he also render in a similar order the first part of the *Principles* and prefix it to the others so that the material, set forth from its proper beginning, might be more pleasing and better understood. Seeing that this was argued very reasonably, he refused to deny the pleas of a friend and the advantage of the reader; and he committed the entire labor of editing and printing to my care, since he lives in the country, far from town, and could not be present.

These, then, worthy reader, are the things that we give you in this little book: the first and second parts of René Descartes' *Principles of Philosophy,* with a fragment of the third; and in addition, as an Appendix, the author's "Thoughts on Metaphysics." But although we mention the first part of the *Principles,* and the title of this book promises it, we do not claim that everything which Descartes said there is exhibited and arranged here in geometrical order; the name has been taken from what is more important in it, and so the principal topics relating to metaphysics, which Descartes handled there and in his *Meditations,* are brought together in this part, while all other matters which belong to logic or are narrated and surveyed only historically are omitted. To accomplish this more easily our author has included in this work almost everything that Descartes arranged in geometrical fashion at the end of the "Reply to the Second Set of Objections." He has begun with all of Descartes' definitions and has inserted Descartes' propositions among his own. Descartes' axioms, however, are not subjoined immediately to the definitions but are postponed until after the fourth proposition, and their order is changed so that they may be more easily demonstrated. Some of Descartes' material, which he did not need, has been omitted. Although it does not escape our author that these axioms can be demonstrated like theorems (as Descartes himself claims in Postulate VII), and although we urged him to treat them as such, still the more important affairs in which he was involved allowed him only two weeks' leisure to finish this work, and consequently he was unable to satisfy his own and our desire. But, while going so far as to add to each axiom a brief explanation to serve in place of a demonstration, he puts off a complete and better demonstration for another time, if perchance a new edition should follow this abridged one. For a new expanded edition we will try to persuade him to complete the entire third part on the visible universe; here we give only the fragment with which our author finished his exposition, for we would not deprive the reader of it, small as it is. If the third part is to be properly completed, several propositions regarding the nature and properties of fluids will have to be interspersed in the second part, and I shall urge the author in every way I can to carry this out at that time.

Our author very often departs from Descartes, not only in his rearrangement and explanation of the axioms, but also in his demonstration of the propositions and in some of the conclusions, and he uses a method of proof very different from that of Descartes. No one should suppose from this that he wanted to correct that distinguished man; rather, it was done to keep to the order already undertaken and to avoid too much increase in the number of axioms. For the same reason he was compelled to demonstrate many things which Descartes had proposed without demonstration, and to add others which Descartes had obviously omitted.

But, above all, I would observe that in the entire work—in

Parts One and Two of the *Principles* together with the fragment of the third, and in his own "Thoughts on Metaphysics" as well—our author has propounded the genuine opinions of Descartes and their demonstrations, either as they are found in his writings or as they should be deduced by a legitimate sequence from the principles he laid down. Since our author had promised to teach his pupil the philosophy of Descartes, he scrupulously refused to depart a finger's breadth from Descartes' opinions or to teach anything which did not correspond to his doctrines or was contrary to them. For although he thinks some of these doctrines are true and although he admits that he has added some of his own, still many doctrines appear which he rejects as false, and in place of them he favors opinions that are far different. Of this sort, to mention one of many, are the statements about will in the Scholium to Proposition XV, Part One of the *Principles* and in Chapter XII, Part Two of the Appendix, even though they seem to be satisfactorily proved with great care and completeness. For he does not think that will is distinct from intellect, much less that it is endowed with that kind of liberty. Descartes, in asserting these things, only supposes and does not prove that human mind is absolutely thinking substance, as is clear from the *Discourse on Method,* Part Four, from the *Meditations,* Part Two, and in other places. Our author, on the contrary, while admitting that there is thinking substance in nature, denies that it constitutes the essence of human mind; he maintains, rather, that just as no limits determine extension, so too no limits determine thought. Accordingly, just as human body is not absolute extension, but only extension specifically determined through motion and rest according to the laws of extended nature, so also human mind or soul does not exist absolutely, but only as thought specifically determined through ideas according to the laws of thinking nature [*per leges Naturae cogitantis*]. Human mind, he concludes, necessarily exists when human body begins to exist. From this definition he thinks there is little difficulty in demonstrating that will is not distinct from intellect, and even less difficulty in demonstrating that will is not capable of the freedom which Descartes ascribes to it. Indeed, he thinks that the faculty of affirming and denying is purely fictitious; that affirmation and negation are nothing apart from ideas; and that the other faculties, such as intellect, desire, and so forth, ought to be classed as fictions or, at least, among the notions which men have formed by conceiving a thing abstractly, like notions of humanity, stoniness, and things of that sort.

Neither should it be overlooked that many assertions which are found in various places should be taken in the same sense as above, that is, as expressing the mind of Descartes: for example, the assertion that "this or that exceeds human grasp." This statement in particular should not be taken as though our author offered it as his own opinion. For he thinks that all such things and others even more sublime and subtle not only can be conceived by us clearly and distinctly, but also can be very conveniently explained, if only human intellect is brought to the investigation of truth and the knowledge of things by a way different from that discovered and followed by Descartes. Thus he thinks that the foundations of knowledge laid by Descartes and the things erected upon them do not suffice for unraveling and solving all the difficult questions occurring in metaphysics, but that other foundations are required if we wish to elevate our intellect to the very summit of knowledge.

Finally (to make an end of prefacing) we want our readers to know that all these treatises are published for no other purpose than the discovery and propagation of truth and to urge men to the study of true and sincere philosophy. Accordingly, all who wish to pluck the ripe fruit we heartily wish for them are cautioned, before girding for the reading, to insert omissions carefully in their proper places and to correct accurately the typographical errors that have crept in. For some of these could present obstacles to the proper understanding of the force of a demonstration and of the author's intention, as anyone may easily see by inspecting them.

THE PRINCIPLES OF THE
PHILOSOPHY OF RENÉ DESCARTES,
DEMONSTRATED IN THE GEOMETRICAL
MANNER

PART ONE

PROLEGOMENON

Before we approach the propositions and their demonstrations it seems wise to set before ourselves briefly why Descartes doubted everything, how he laid the solid foundations of the sciences, and, finally, by what means he liberated himself from all doubts. All this we would have reduced to mathematical order had we not decided that the prolixity required for setting it out might prevent these matters being rightly understood, since they ought to be seen at a glance as in a painting.

Descartes, then, in order to proceed with all caution in investigating, attempted:

To set aside all prejudices.
To find the foundations upon which everything else might be erected.
To reveal the cause of error.
To understand all things clearly and distinctly.

In order to secure his first, second, and third aims, he undertook to reduce everything to doubt, not like a skeptic who apprehends no other end than doubt itself, but in order to free his mind from all prejudice. Thus he hoped to discover the firm and unshakable foundations of science, which, if there were any, could not escape him as he followed this method. For the true principles of knowledge should be so clear and certain as to need no proof, should be placed beyond all hazard of doubt, and should be such that nothing could be proved without them. After a long period of doubt he discovered them. Then, after he had discovered the principles, it was not difficult for him to distinguish true from false and to expose the cause of error, and, accordingly, to prevent himself from taking something false and doubtful as true and certain.

To secure his fourth and final aim, that is, to understand all things clearly and distinctly, his principal rule was to enumerate all the simple ideas of which all other ideas are composed, and to examine each of them individually. For when he could perceive the simple ideas clearly and distinctly, without doubt he could also understand with the same clarity and distinctness all other ideas made up of these simple ones.

With this by way of introduction, we shall now explain briefly how he reduced all things to doubt, how he discovered the true principles of knowledge, and how he extricated himself from the difficulties caused by his doubts.

1. *Doubting all things.* First he calls to mind all the things he had received through his senses, such as the sky, the earth, and the like, and his own body as well, all of which he had regarded until then as existing in nature. Then he doubts the certainty of these things, because he had observed that his senses sometimes deceived him; also, because in sleep he had often persuaded himself that certain things really existed outside himself, although afterward he recognized that he had been deluded; and finally, because he had heard others, competent people, assert that they sensed a pain in parts of their bodies which they had lost. In this way he could, not unreasonably, doubt even the existence of his own body. From all these considerations he could then rightly conclude that the senses are not a sufficiently firm foundation upon which to rest all knowledge (for they could be brought into doubt), but that certitude must depend on other principles which we find more sure. In order to investigate these, he sets before himself next all universal qualities, such as corporeal nature in general, and its extension, figure, quantity, and so forth, as well as all mathematical truths. Although these appeared more certain to him than the things he had received through the senses, yet he found a reason for doubting them, because, to be sure, others were in error about such things, but chiefly because an opinion had long been established in his mind that God exists, who can do all things, and who created him exactly as he is, and who, accordingly, had perhaps made him

to be deceived in those very things which seemed clearest to him. Such then is the manner in which he reduced everything to doubt.

2. *Discovery of the foundation of all knowledge.* But to find the true principles of the sciences, he next inquired whether he might doubt everything that could fall within his thought, so as to discover whether perhaps something was left which he had not yet doubted. For if, after all this doubting, anything remained which he could not doubt for any of his previous reasons or in any other way, such a thing, he rightly judged, would have to be chosen as the foundation upon which he would erect all his knowledge. Now, although he seemed to have doubted everything already, both the things taken in through his senses and the things perceived solely through his intellect, there still remained something which had to be considered, namely, himself who was doing the doubting, not as consisting of head, hands, and other corporeal members, since he had doubted these, but only so far as he doubted, thought, and so forth. Examining this carefully, he saw that he could not doubt this for any of his previous reasons. For whether he thinks while dreaming or awake, still he thinks, and is; and although others as well as himself had been in error about different things, still because they were in error, they were. Nor could he suppose that the author of his nature was so skilled as to deceive him in this, since it must be allowed that he exists as long as he is supposed to be deceived. Finally, no other cause of doubt could be conceived but that it would at the same time make him entirely certain of his own existence. In short, the more reasons there are for doubting, the more arguments there are to convince him of his own existence. Consequently, in whatever direction he turns in his doubting, he is forced to utter these words: "I doubt, I think, therefore I am."

When, therefore, he had detected this truth, he at the same time discovered the foundation of all the sciences, as well as the measure and rule of all other truths, namely, *whatever is perceived as clearly and as distinctly as this is true.*

That only this can be the foundation of the sciences is clear enough from what has been said, since everything else can easily be doubted—but this not at all. However, with regard to this foundation one thing should be especially noted: the statement "I doubt, I think, therefore I am" is not a syllogism in which the major proposition has been omitted. For if it were a syllogism, the premises would have to be clearer and better known than the conclusion *ergo sum;* consequently, *ergo sum* would not be the prime foundation of all knowledge. Besides, it would not be a certain conclusion, for its truth would depend upon universal premises which the author had already thrown into doubt. Therefore, *cogito, ergo sum* is a unique proposition equivalent to "I am a thinking thing" [*ego sum cogitans*].

Further, in order to avoid confusion in what follows we must know (for the matter must be clearly and distinctly perceived) what we are. Once this is clearly and distinctly understood, we shall not confuse our essence with that of others. Therefore, to deduce this from the above, our author continues as follows.

He recollects all the thoughts he formerly had of himself, as that his own soul is something slight like wind, or fire, or ether, infused in the coarser parts of his body; that body is better known to him than soul, and is more clearly and distinctly perceived. He perceives that all these opinions are clearly inconsistent with those he had just come to understand. For he could doubt his own body, but not his own essence so long as he was actually thinking. Also, he did not now perceive these things clearly and distinctly, and according to his prescribed method, he had to reject them as false. Consequently, since he could not understand how such things pertained to himself, as he was now known to himself, he goes on to ask what there is pertaining properly to his own essence that he could not throw into doubt and through which he would be forced to conclude his own existence. But there are such things: for instance, he wanted to guard himself against being deceived; he wanted to understand many things; he doubted everything he could not understand; thus far he affirmed one thing only; everything else he denied and rejected as false; many other things he imagined against his will; finally, he noticed many things coming, it seemed, from his senses. Since from each of these individually he was able with equal evidence to gather his own existence, and could doubt none of them, and since all of these could be conceived under the same attribute, it follows that all these are true and pertain to his nature. And so when he had said *cogito,* all the modes of thinking were understood: doubting, understanding, affirming, denying, willing, refusing, imagining, and sensing.

Here one should especially notice something which will be very useful when the distinction between mind and body is being treated: first, that these modes of thinking are clearly and distinctly understood apart from everything else which can still be doubted; and, second, that the clear and distinct idea we have of these modes is reduced to obscurity and confusion if we are willing to ascribe to them anything of which we are still in doubt.

3. *Liberation from all doubts.* Finally, to remove all doubt and to achieve certainty in those things which he had thrown into doubt, he goes on to inquire into the nature of the most perfect being, and whether such a being exists. For when he discerns that a perfect being exists, by whose force all things are produced and conserved, and for whom it is naturally incompatible to be a deceiver, then that reason for doubting which he had because he was ignorant of his own cause will be destroyed. For he will know that the faculty of distinguishing true and false had not been given to him by a supremely good and truthful God in order that he might be deceived. Accordingly, mathematical truths and everything which seems to him evidently true could by no means be suspect. He proceeds then to remove the other causes of doubt by asking how it comes about that we are sometimes in error. When he discovered that error springs from our using free will to assent to things which we perceive only confusedly, he could at once conclude that he could in the future guard against error

by consenting only to clear and distinct perceptions. Every-one, in fact, can do this, since each has the power of restrain-ing his will and keeping it within the limits of the under-standing. However, because in our youth we absorbed many prejudices from which we are not easily freed, our author, in order that we might be freed of prejudice and embrace nothing but what we clearly and distinctly perceive, goes on to enumerate all the simple notions and ideas from which our thoughts are composed, and then examines them one by one in order to see what is clear and what obscure in each. For in this way he will easily be able to distinguish the clear from the obscure, to form clear and distinct thoughts, and conse-quently to discover the real distinction between mind and body; also, he will find what is clear in things taken in by the senses and what obscure, and, finally, how dreaming dif-fers from wakefulness. Having done this, he could no longer doubt his ideas while awake nor be deceived by his senses. Thus he freed himself of all the doubts considered above.

Before finishing this section, perhaps I ought to satisfy those who argue as follows: Since the existence of God is not known to us through itself, we apparently can never be certain of anything; and we can never know that God exists. For from uncertain premises (since we have said that all things are uncertain so long as we are ignorant of our origin) nothing certain can be concluded.

To remove this difficulty, Descartes replies as follows: Al-though we do not yet know whether the author of our origin has created us to be deceived even in things which appear most evident, still we cannot, on this account, doubt things which we clearly and distinctly understand either in them-selves or through a process of reasoning in which we are actually engaged. We can only doubt things which we have demonstrated heretofore, and which recur to our memory although we no longer contemplate, and have probably for-gotten, the reasons for which we deduced them. So even if the fact that God exists could not be known through itself but only through something else, still we could arrive at a definite knowledge of God's existence by accurately studying the premises from which we conclude his existence. (See the *Principles of Philosophy*, Part I, Principle 13; and "Reply to the Second Set of Objections," Number 3; and also the latter part of "Meditation V.")

However, since this reply may not satisfy everyone, I will give another. We saw above, when we were discussing the certitude and evidence of our existence, that we could infer it from the fact that wherever we turned our minds we found no reason for doubt which did not in itself convince us of our own existence, whether we contemplated our own nature, or supposed the author of our nature to be a skilled deceiver, or, finally, called in from beyond ourselves any reason whatsoever for doubt. Up to this point we see that this certitude of existence is true of nothing else. For although in attending to the nature of a triangle, for instance, we are compelled to conclude that its three angles are equal to two right ones, still, because we may perhaps be deceived by the author of our nature, we cannot conclude this with certainty, whereas from the very possibility of deception we can most certainly infer our own existence. Accordingly, we are not compelled to infer, wherever we look, that the three angles of a triangle are equal to two right angles; on the contrary, we find cause for doubting it, since we possess no true idea of God which would make it impossible for us to think that he may be a deceiver. It is just as easy for a person who has no true idea of God (as we suppose, for the moment, to be our own case) to think that his author is a deceiver, as not a deceiver; similarly, for a person who has no idea of a triangle, it is equally easy to think that the three angles of a triangle are not equal to two right angles, as to think that they are. Therefore, we grant that besides our own existence we can be absolutely certain of nothing, however carefully we attend to its demonstration, so long as we have no clear and distinct concept of God which enables us to affirm that God is absolutely truthful, just as the idea we have of a triangle compels us to conclude that its three angles are equal to two right angles. But we deny that this prevents our arriving at some knowledge. For, as is obvious from everything that has already been said, the pivot of the entire matter is this, that we can form a concept of God which so disposes us that we cannot with equal ease suppose that he is a deceiver as that he is not, but which compels us to affirm that he is entirely truthful. But when we have formed such an idea, the reason for doubting mathematical truths is removed. For then wherever we turn our minds in order to doubt any one of these things, just as in the case of our own existence, we find nothing to prevent our concluding that it is entirely certain. For instance, if after the idea of God has been discovered we consider the nature of a triangle, the idea of it compels us to affirm that its three angles are equal to two right angles; but if we consider the idea of God, this idea too compels us to affirm that he is the entirely truthful author and continual preserver of our nature, and accordingly does not deceive us in regard to this truth. When we consider the idea of God (which we suppose we have now discovered), it will be no less impossible for us to think that he is a deceiver than, in considering the idea of a triangle, to think that its three angles are not equal to two right ones. Just as we can form such an idea of a triangle even though we do not know whether the author of our nature deceives us, so also we can make the idea of God clear to ourselves and present to our minds even though we may still doubt whether the author of our nature deceives us entirely. Provided only we have this idea, however we acquire it, it will suffice to remove every doubt, as has already been shown. With these considerations in mind, I reply to the proposed difficulty: we can be certain of nothing, not indeed while we are ignorant of God's existence (for we have not spoken of this matter), but while we have no clear and distinct idea of him. Therefore, if anyone should wish to argue against me, his argument will have to run as follows: we can be certain of nothing before we have a clear and distinct idea of God. But we cannot have a clear and distinct idea of God so long as we do not know whether the author of our nature deceives us. Therefore, we can be certain of nothing so long as we do not know whether the author of our nature deceives us, and so forth. To this I reply by granting the major and denying the minor. For we have a clear and distinct idea of a triangle, although we do not know whether the author of our nature deceives us; and provided we have such an idea of God as we have just now described, we cannot doubt his existence, and we cannot doubt any mathematical truth.

With this for a preface, we now turn to the subject itself.

DEFINITIONS TAKEN FROM DESCARTES [1]

1. Under the word *thought* I include everything that exists in us in such a way that we are immediately conscious of it.

Thus all the operations of will, understanding, imagination, and sense are thoughts. But I have added the word *immediately* so as to exclude consequences of such operations; for example, voluntary movement does indeed have thought as its principle, but even so it is not thought.

2. By the word *idea* I understand the form of a thought, through the immediate perception of which I am conscious of that particular thought.

So long as I understand what I say, I cannot express anything in words without thereby being assured that the idea signified by these words exists in me. Thus, images depicted in the fancy are not the only things that I call ideas. In fact, so far as such images exist only in corporeal fancy—that is, when such images are only depicted in some part of the brain

[1] [Spinoza takes these definitions almost word for word from Descartes' geometrical demonstrations of the existence of God at the end of the "Reply to the Second Set of Objections." But where Descartes had included both definition and explanatory remarks in a single paragraph, Spinoza sets the definition apart and makes an additional paragraph of the explanatory material. Spinoza also adds a note to Def. 4 and omits in the explanation of Def. 5 Descartes' observation that nothing real can be attributed to nothing.]

—I do not call them ideas at all; rather, only insofar as they inform the mind itself when it is turned toward that part of the brain do I call such images ideas.

3. By the *objective reality of an idea* I understand so much of the being of a thing [*entitatem rei*] as is represented through an idea and exists in the idea.

Similarly, it can be called the objective perfection of an idea, or objective artifice [*artificium objectivum*], and so forth. For all that we perceive as being in the objects of ideas is in the ideas themselves objectively.

4. Things are said to be in the objects of ideas *formally,* when they are the same in the objects as they are in our perceptions. And they are in the objects *eminently,* when they are not actually such as we perceive them, but are of such force that they can be substituted for things as we actually perceive them.

Notice that when I say a cause contains the perfections of its effect *eminently,* I mean that the cause contains the perfections of its effect more excellently than the effect itself. (See Axiom 8.)

5. Everything in which anything is immediately contained, as in a subject, or through which anything that we perceive exists—that is, any property, or quality, or attribute of which we have in ourselves a real idea—is called *substance.*

For we have no other idea of substance itself, taken precisely, than that it is a thing in which this something that we perceive or this something that is objectively in one of our ideas, exists formally or eminently.

6. Substance in which thought is immediately contained is called *mind.*

I speak here of mind [*mens*] rather than of soul [*anima*] because the word *soul* is equivocal and is often used for a corporeal thing.

7. Substance which is the immediate subject of extension and of the accidents that presuppose extension, like figure, place, local motion, and so forth, is called *body* [*corpus*].

Whether mind and body are one and the same substance, or two different substances, must be considered later.

8. Substance which we understand to be supremely perfect through itself and in which we conceive nothing that involves any defect or limitation of perfection is called *God*.

9. To say that anything is contained in the nature or concept of a thing is the same as saying that it is true of this thing or can be truly affirmed of it.

10. Two substances are said to be really distinct when each of them can exist without the other.

I omit here Descartes' postulates since no conclusions are drawn from them in what follows. However, I strongly urge the reader to go through them all and to study them with thoughtful attention.

AXIOMS [2]

1. We do not arrive at knowledge and certainty of an unknown thing except through knowledge and certainty of something else which is itself prior in certainty and knowledge.

2. There are reasons which make us doubt the existence of our own bodies.

This was made clear in the Prolegomenon, and so it is included here simply as an axiom.

3. If we have anything in us other than mind and body, it is less known to us than mind and body.

Notice that these axioms affirm nothing of things external to us, but affirm only the things which we discover in ourselves so far as we are thinking things.

---

[2] [These first three axioms are not taken from Descartes, but are supplied by Spinoza for convenience of exposition. Nevertheless, as we are told in Louis Meyer's Preface, Spinoza insists that supplements of this sort represent the genuine opinions of Descartes "either as they are found in his writings or as they should be deduced by a legitimate sequence from the principles he laid down" (Louis Meyer's Preface, p. 8).]

PROPOSITION I [3]

We can be absolutely certain of nothing, so long as we do not know that we ourselves exist.

Demonstration. This proposition is self-evident. For a man who simply does not know that he exists, at the same time does not know that he exists as a being who affirms or denies: that is, he does not know what he affirms with certainty or denies with certainty.

Notice here, however, that although we affirm and deny many things with great certainty while not noticing the fact that we exist, still unless this fact is presupposed beyond all doubt, everything can be reduced to doubt.

PROPOSITION II

Ego sum must be known through itself.

Demonstration. If you deny the proposition, this statement *ego sum* will become known only through something else, the knowledge and certainty of which will (by Axiom 1) be in us prior to the statement *ego sum.* But this is absurd (by the preceding proposition); therefore, it must be known through itself.—Q.E.D.

PROPOSITION III

Ego, as a thing consisting of body, *sum,* is not the first thing known, and is not known through itself.

Demonstration. There are certain things which make us doubt the existence of our bodies (by Axiom 2); therefore (by Axiom 1), we do not arrive at knowledge and certainty of our bodies

[3] [Like the preceding axioms, Propositions I through IV are not taken from the "Reply to the Second Set of Objections," but are supplied by Spinoza for convenience of exposition.]

except through knowledge and certainty of something else which is itself prior in certainty and knowledge. Therefore, this statement, *"ego,* as a thing consisting of body, *sum,"* is not the first thing known and is not known through itself.—Q.E.D.

PROPOSITION IV

Ego sum cannot be the first thing known except insofar as we are actually thinking.

Demonstration. This statement, "I am a corporeal thing or a thing consisting of body," is not the first thing known (by the preceding proposition); also, I am not certain of my own existence so far as I consist of anything more than mind and body; for if we consist of anything different from mind and body, that other thing is less known to us than body (by Axiom 3). Consequently, *ego sum* cannot be the first thing known except insofar as we are thinking.—Q.E.D.

COROLLARY

Hence, it is obvious that mind or thinking thing is better known than body.

However, for a more complete explanation read Principles 11 and 12 in Part One of the *Principles.*

SCHOLIUM

Everyone perceives with certainty that he affirms, denies, doubts, understands, imagines, and so forth; or, that he exists doubting, understanding, affirming, and so forth; or, in a word, that he exists *thinking;* and he cannot doubt these things. Therefore, this statement, *cogito* or *sum cogitans,* is the unique (by Proposition I) and entirely certain foundation of all philosophy. Now since in the sciences nothing more is to be sought or desired to make us certain about things than that all things be deduced from firm principles and be made as clear and distinct as the principles from which they are deduced, it follows clearly that everything must be taken as absolutely true which is just as evident to us and is perceived as clearly and distinctly as the principle we have now discovered—everything, in fact, which agrees with this principle and is so dependent upon it that if we wanted to doubt it, we would have to doubt the principle too. However, to proceed as cautiously as possible in recounting these things, I will at first admit as being perceived with equal evidence, clarity, and distinctness only such things as each person observes in himself while he thinks; for example, that he wills this and that, that he has ideas of a definite kind, that one idea contains more reality and perfection than another, that the idea which contains objectively the being and perfection of substance is far more perfect than the idea which contains only the objective perfection of some accident, that the most perfect of all these is the idea of absolutely perfect being. Such things, I say, we perceive not only with equal evidence and clarity, but with perhaps even greater distinctness. For they not only affirm that we think, but also how we think. Moreover, we will say that those things also agree with our fundamental principle, which cannot be doubted without at the same time throwing our unshakable foundation into doubt; as, for instance, if anyone wanted to doubt whether something can come from nothing, he could at the same time doubt that we ourselves exist while we are actually thinking. For if I can affirm anything of nothing, in the sense that "nothing" can be the cause of something, I can at the same time and with equal right affirm thought of nothing and say that I am nothing while I am thinking. But since I find this impossible, it will also be impossible for me to think that something comes from nothing.

After these considerations I have decided to introduce here certain things which at present seem necessary to our further progress, and to add them to our group of axioms, seeing that they were proposed as axioms by Descartes toward the end of the "Reply to the Second Set of Objections," and since I have no desire to be more accurate than he was. Yet, so as not to depart from the order already undertaken, I shall attempt to present them more clearly, and to show how one depends upon another and all upon the principle *ego sum cogitans,* or how they evidently and reasonably agree with this principle.

AXIOMS TAKEN FROM DESCARTES [4]

4. There are different grades of reality or entity; for substance has more reality than accident or mode, and infinite substance more than finite, so that there is more objective reality in the idea of substance than in the idea of accident, and more in the idea of infinite substance than in the idea of finite substance.

This axiom is known solely from the contemplation of our ideas, of whose existence we are certain, because they are modes of thinking, for we know how much reality or perfection the idea of substance affirms of substance, and how much also the idea of mode affirms of mode. This being so, we necessarily see that the idea of substance contains more objective reality than the idea of accident, and so forth. (See the Scholium to Proposition IV.)

5. If a thinking thing comes to know of any perfections that it lacks, it will at once give them to itself if they are in its power.

[4] [In attempting to present Descartes' axioms "more clearly," Spinoza has simplified them by omitting Descartes' explanatory remarks and has modified them by changing the wording slightly. In order to show how "one depends upon another and all upon the principle *ego sum cogitans,*" he has rearranged their order. The correspondence between the two sets is as follows:

Spinoza	Descartes	Spinoza	Descartes
Axiom 4	Axiom 6	Axiom 8	Axiom 4
5	7	9	5
6	10	10	2
7	3	11	1

Descartes' Axioms 8 and 9, omitted from this arrangement, are introduced and discussed later in the Scholium to Proposition VII.

In each case, Spinoza states the axiom in the first paragraph and adds his promised explanation in the paragraph or paragraphs that follow.]

Everyone, to the extent that he is a thinking thing, observes this in himself; consequently (by the Scholium to Proposition IV), we are entirely certain of it, and by the same cause we are no less certain of the following:

6. Either possible or necessary existence is contained in the idea or concept of every thing. (See Descartes' Axiom 10.)

Existence is necessary in the concept of God or of a being supremely perfect, for otherwise he would be thought of as imperfect, which is contrary to the supposition. Existence is contingent, or possible, in the concept of a limited thing.

7. There is no thing, nor any perfection of a thing, actually existing which can have nothing, or a nonexisting thing, as the cause of its existence.

I demonstrated in the Scholium to Proposition IV that this axiom is as evident as the statement *ego sum cogitans*.

8. Whatever reality or perfection there is in a thing exists either formally or eminently in its first and adequate cause.

By *eminently* I mean that the cause contains the whole reality of the effect more perfectly than the effect itself; by *formally* I mean that the effect contains that reality with equal perfection.

This axiom depends on the preceding one, for on the supposition that there is *nothing* in the cause or *less* in the cause than in the effect, nothing in the cause would be the cause of the effect. But this is absurd (by the preceding axiom); consequently, the cause of an effect cannot be anything one pleases, but precisely that which contains eminently, or at least formally, the entire perfection which exists in the effect.

9. The objective reality of our ideas requires a cause in which this same reality is contained not only objectively, but formally or eminently.

This axiom is acknowledged by everyone, although many have misused it. For when anyone has thought of something new, there is no one who does not ask the cause of his concept or idea. When they can truly assign some cause that contains formally or eminently as much reality as exists objectively in that concept, they are satisfied. This is sufficiently explained through the example of the machine which Descartes introduces in Principle 17, Part One of the *Principles*. Similarly, if anyone should ask from what source a man has the ideas of his own thought and body, no one fails to see that he has them from himself, seeing that he contains at least formally everything that the ideas contain objectively. For this reason, if a man should have an idea which has more objective reality than he has formal reality, we, impelled by the Natural Light,[5] will necessarily seek outside that man another cause which contains all this perfection formally or eminently. But no one has ever assigned a cause additional to one that he has conceived with equal clarity and distinctness.

The truth of this axiom, we might add, depends on what has preceded. For (by Axiom 4) there are different grades of reality or entity in ideas, and for this reason (by Axiom 8) in proportion to their grade of perfection they require a more perfect cause. In fact, since the grades of reality [6] which we see in ideas are not in the ideas, considered simply as modes of thinking, but rather are in the ideas so far as one represents substance, or another simply a mode of substance, or, in a word, inasmuch as they are considered as images of things, it clearly follows that no first cause of ideas can exist other than that which, as we have just shown, everyone clearly and distinctly understands through the Natural Light: namely, that cause which contains formally or eminently the very same reality which ideas possess objectively. To clarify this conclusion I will illustrate it by several examples. First, if a person looks at several books (suppose one to be the work of a distinguished philosopher, another that of some trifler) written in the same hand, and does not regard the sense of the words (that is, does not take them as images) but notices only the delineation of the characters and the order of the

---

5 [By the "Natural Light" (*Lumen Naturale*), Descartes usually means our innate faculty of knowing, uncorrupted by prejudice and unilluminated by Scripture.]

6 We are also certain of this, because we see it in ourselves while thinking. See Prop. IV, Scholium.

letters, he will see no disparity between the books which would lead him to look for different causes, but they will seem to have proceeded from the same cause in the same manner. But if he attends to the sense of the words and the discourse, he will discover a great disparity between them, and from that will conclude that the first cause of the one book was far different from the first cause of the other and that the one cause was more perfect than the other in proportion as the sense of the discourse in each book or as the words considered as images differ from one another. I speak of a first cause of the books, which must necessarily exist, even though I grant and really suppose that one book can, obviously, be copied from another. The same conclusion can also be clearly explained through the example of a portrait, say of some prince. For if we consider only its materials we will discover between this portrait and others no disparity which would compel us to look for different causes; indeed, nothing will prevent our thinking that this portrait was painted from one image, that image from another, and so ad infinitum. For we discern well enough that no other cause is required for its delineation. But if we think of the image as an image, we are at once driven to seek a first cause which contains formally or eminently what the image contains by representation. I do not see what more might be desired for establishing and explaining this axiom.

10. No less a cause is required to conserve a thing than was required to produce it in the first place.

From the fact that we are at this moment thinking, it does not follow necessarily that we shall think hereafter. For the concept that we have of our thought does not entail or does not contain the necessary existence of thought; for I can conceive thought clearly and distinctly [7] even though I suppose it does not exist. Since, however, the nature of any cause ought to contain or involve in itself the perfection of its own effect (by Axiom 8), it clearly follows that either in us or beyond us there exists necessarily at this very moment something

[7] Everyone, to the extent that he is a thinking thing, sees this in himself.

which we have not yet understood, whose concept or nature involves existence, and which is the cause of our thought's beginning to exist and, also, of its continuing to exist. For, although our thought has begun to exist, its nature and essence do not on that account involve necessary existence more than before it existed, so that it needs the same force to persevere in existence that it needs to come into existence. This fact, which we assert of thought, is to be asserted also of everything whose essence does not entail necessary existence.

11. Nothing exists of which it cannot be asked what the cause (or reason) is of its existing. (See Descartes' Axiom 1.)

Since to exist is a positive thing, we cannot say that existence has nothing for its cause (by Axiom 7); therefore, we must assign some positive cause or reason for the existence of a thing—either an external cause, that is, one which exists externally to the thing itself, or an internal cause, that is, one which is comprehended in the nature and definition of the existing thing itself.

FOUR PROPOSITIONS TAKEN FROM DESCARTES [8]

PROPOSITION V

The existence of God is known solely from the consideration of his nature.

Demonstration. To say that something is contained in the nature or concept of a thing is the same as saying that it is true of this thing (by Definition 9). But necessary existence is

[8] [The propositions are taken from the "Reply to the Second Set of Objections"; the scholia are added by Spinoza. The correspondence between the two sets is as follows:

	Spinoza	*Descartes*
	Proposition V	Proposition I
	VI	II
	VII	III
	VIII	IV

In Proposition VII Spinoza criticizes Descartes' demonstration of Proposition III and offers a radically modified proof.]

contained in the concept of God (by Axiom 6). Therefore, it is true to say of God that necessary existence is in him, or that he exists.

SCHOLIUM

From this proposition many notable things follow: from the fact that existence pertains to the nature of God, or that the concept of God involves necessary existence just as the concept of a triangle involves the fact that its three angles are equal to two right angles, or that his existence no less than his essence is an eternal truth—upon this alone depends almost all our knowledge of the attributes of God, through which we are led to the love of God (that is, to our utmost beatitude). This is why it would be so desirable for mankind sometime, finally, to share these views with us. I admit, of course, that certain prejudices [9] exist which prevent people from readily understanding this. But if anyone, led solely by the love of truth and his own true advantage, is willing to examine the matter equitably and to weigh with himself the things which are dealt with in the "Fifth Meditation" and toward the end of the "Reply to the First Set of Objections," as well as those concerning eternity which we discuss in Part Two, Chapter I of the Appendix, he undoubtedly will understand the matter as clearly as possible, and no one will be able to doubt that he has some idea of God (which truly is the ultimate foundation of human beatitude). For he will clearly see that the idea of God differs widely from the ideas of other things as soon as he understands that God, both in essence and existence, is entirely and generically different from everything else. And so there is no need to keep the reader longer on these things.

PROPOSITION VI

The existence of God is demonstrated a posteriori solely from the fact that the idea of God exists in us.

9 Read *Principles*, Part I, Prin. 16.

Demonstration. The objective reality of any of our ideas requires a cause in which the same reality is contained not only objectively, but formally or eminently (by Axiom 9). But we have an idea of God (by Definitions 2 and 8), and the objective reality of this idea is not contained in us either formally or eminently (by Axiom 4), and it cannot be contained in anything else but God himself (by Definition 8). Therefore, the idea of God which is in us requires God for its cause, and consequently (by Axiom 7) God exists.

SCHOLIUM

There are some who deny that they have any idea of God, whom, nevertheless, they claim to worship and love. And even if you put the definition of God and the attributes of God before their eyes, you will accomplish nothing; no more, by Hercules, than if you labored to teach a man blind from birth the differences in colors as we see them. But unless we are willing to regard these people as a new kind of animal, midway between men and brutes, we should pay little attention to their words. How else, I ask, can we bring the idea of a thing into plain view than by giving its definition and explaining its attributes? But since we do just this with regard to the idea of God, there is no reason for us to be troubled by the words of men who deny God simply because they can form no image of him in their brains.

Notice also that when Descartes cites Axiom Four to show that the objective reality of the idea of God is not contained in us formally or eminently, he supposes that everyone knows that he is not himself infinite substance, that is, supremely intelligent, supremely powerful, and so forth. Descartes can suppose this, since everyone who realizes that he thinks also realizes that he is in doubt about many things and does not understand everything clearly and distinctly.

Finally, one should also notice that it clearly follows from Definition Eight that there cannot exist many Gods, but only

one, as we clearly demonstrate in Proposition XI of this part
and in Part Two, Chapter II of our Appendix.

PROPOSITION VII

The existence of God is also demonstrated from the fact that
we ourselves, who have the idea of him, exist.

SCHOLIUM

To demonstrate this proposition Descartes assumes two
axioms, namely: (1) That which can accomplish a greater or
more difficult thing can also accomplish a thing which is less
difficult. (2) It is greater to create or (by Axiom 10) to conserve substance than to create or to conserve the attributes or
properties of substance. What he means by these axioms I do
not know. For what does he call easy, or what difficult? Nothing is called easy or difficult absolutely,[10] but only in respect
of a cause, so that one and the same thing, at the same time,
can be called easy and difficult in respect of different causes.
But if he calls things difficult which can be done by a particular cause only with great labor, and things easy which can
be done by the same cause with less labor—as, for instance, a
force which can lift fifty pounds can lift twenty-five pounds
twice as easily—this axiom will not be true absolutely, and he
will not be able to demonstrate from it what he intends. For
when he says, "If I had the power of conserving myself, I
should also have the power to endow myself with all the
perfections which are lacking in me" (because these do not in
fact require so great a force), I would agree that these powers
which I expend in my conservation could accomplish many
other things far more easily, if I did not need them to conserve
my being, but so long as I do use them in conserving my being, I do not agree that I can devote them to accomplishing

[10] In lieu of other examples, consider the example of the spider who
easily weaves a web which men would weave only with the greatest difficulty; men, on the other hand, do many things quite easily which, perhaps,
are impossible for angels.

other things, even though easier, as is clearly seen in our example. Nor does it remove the difficulty to say that since I am a thinking thing, I ought necessarily to know whether I expend all my strength in conserving myself, and also whether this is the reason that I do not endow myself with other perfections. Actually (apart from the fact that this new consideration is not now in dispute, our concern being only to know whether Proposition VII follows necessarily from this axiom), if I should know all this, I would then be greater than I now am and would perhaps require greater powers than I now possess in order to conserve myself in that greater perfection. Further, I do not know whether it is a greater task to create (or conserve) substance than to create attributes; that is, to speak more clearly and philosophically, I do not know whether substance does not need, in order to conserve its attributes, the entire virtue and essence by which it conserves itself. But let us leave this and examine more closely what our author intends here: what does he mean by *easily* and *with difficulty?* I do not think, and in no way persuade myself, that by *with difficulty* he means that which is impossible (for then it would be by no means possible to conceive how a thing comes about), and that by *easily* he means that which implies no contradiction (for then it is easily conceived how a thing comes about); although in the "Third Meditation" he seems at first glance to mean this when he says, "Nor should I suppose that the things which are lacking in me are perhaps more difficult to acquire than those which are already in me. For, on the contrary, it is manifest that it was far more difficult that I, a thinking thing or substance, should emerge from nothing, than, and so forth." For this neither agrees with our author's words nor smacks of his genius. For, to omit the first point, between the possible and the impossible or between what is intelligible and what is not intelligible there is no common measure, just as there is none between something and nothing; power [*potestas*] is no more predicated of impossibilities than creation and generation are of non-entities; consequently, they must not be compared in any way with one another. Add, too, that I can compare and get to know relations only among things of which I have a clear and distinct concept. I deny therefore this sequence, that he who can do the impossible can also do what is possible. For, I ask, what sort of conclusion would the following be: if anyone can make a square circle, he can also make a circle of which all the lines that can be drawn from the center to the circumference are equal, or, if anyone can manipulate *nothing* and use it as a material from which to produce something, he will also have the power to produce something out of something? For, as I said, between these and similar things there is no agreement, no analogy, no comparison, and no proportion whatsoever. Anyone can see this if he will consider it a bit. And so I believe that such an interpretation is entirely foreign to Descartes' genius. But if I consider the second of the two axioms just adduced, it seems that by *greater* and *more difficult* Descartes means that which is more perfect, but by *less* and *more easily* that which is more imperfect. And this too seems very obscure. There is the same difficulty here as above. For, as above, I deny that he who can do more can at the same time and in the same work do less, but this has to be supposed in the proposition. Then, when he says, "It is greater to create or conserve substance than it is attributes," obviously he cannot mean by attributes that which is contained in substance formally and is distinct from substance only in reason. For in this case it is one and the same thing to create substance and to create its attributes. And also, for the same reason, he cannot mean the properties of substance, which follow necessarily from its essence and definition. Much less can he mean, although it seems to be his intention, the properties and attributes of another substance: as, for instance, if I say that I have the power to conserve myself as a finite thinking substance, I cannot for that reason say that I also have the power of endowing myself with all the perfections of an infinite substance, which differs entirely from my essence. For the force or essence by which I conserve myself [11]

[11] Notice that the force by which substance conserves itself is nothing more than its essence and does not differ from it except in name; this will be a principal topic when in the Appendix we treat of the power of God.

in being differs totally and generically from the force or essence by which absolutely infinite substance conserves itself,
since such a substance and its powers and properties are to be
distinguished only in reason. Consequently (even on the assumption that I myself conserve myself), if I should suppose
that I can endow myself with the perfections of absolutely
infinite substance, I would be supposing nothing other than
that I can reduce my entire being to nothing and can create
infinite substance entirely anew. This, obviously, would be
far more than to suppose simply that I can conserve myself as
finite substance. And so, since he cannot mean by attributes or
properties any of the foregoing things, nothing remains but
the qualities which substance contains in itself eminently (as,
in mind, this or that thought which I clearly perceive is want-
ing in me), but not the qualities which a different substance
contains eminently (as, in extension, this or that motion, for
such perfections are not perfections in me as a thinking thing
and consequently are not lacking in me). But then what Descartes wants to demonstrate can in no way be inferred from
this axiom, namely, that if I conserve myself I also have the
power to endow myself with all the perfection that I clearly
see belongs to a being supremely perfect. This is evident
enough from what has just been said. However, so as not to
leave the matter unproved and to avoid all confusion, it
seemed fitting to us first to demonstrate the following lemmas
and then to base on them the demonstration of Proposition
VII.

LEMMA 1

In proportion as a thing is by its own nature more perfect, it
entails a greater and more necessary existence; and, conversely,
in proportion as a thing entails by its own nature a more
necessary existence, the more perfect it is.

Demonstration. Existence is contained in the idea or concept
of every thing (by Axiom 6). Suppose then that there is a thing
A which has ten degrees of perfection: by this I mean that the

concept of A entails more existence than if A were supposed to contain only five degrees of perfection. For, since we cannot affirm existence of nothing (see the Scholium to Proposition IV), the more we take away in thought from the perfection of A, and thus perceive that it participates more and more in nothing, to that extent we deny it the possibility of existence. And so, if we conceive its degrees of perfection as being infinitely reduced, that is, diminished to zero, A will contain no existence or absolutely impossible existence. If, on the other hand, we increase its degrees of being to infinity, we will think that it involves the utmost existence and consequently that it is utterly necessary. This was our first point. Then, since these two [necessary existence and perfection] can in no way be separated (as is sufficiently evident from Axiom 6 and from the entire first part of this demonstration), the second part of our proposition clearly follows.

Note I: Although many things are said to exist necessarily simply because a sufficient [*determinata*] cause exists for their production, we are not speaking of such things here, but only of that necessity and possibility which follow solely from a consideration of the nature or essence of a thing, without regard to a cause.

Note II: We do not speak here of beauty and the other perfections which men have wanted, through superstition and ignorance, to call perfections.[12] By perfection I mean only reality or being. For example, I perceive that there is in substance more reality than in modes or accidents, and consequently I know clearly that substance contains an existence more necessary and more perfect than accidents, as is sufficiently evident from Axioms Four and Six.

COROLLARY

Hence it follows that whatever entails necessary existence is entirely perfect being, or God.

[12] [Spinoza's phrasing. The text reads (Van Vloten edn., 130): "hic non loquimur de pulchritudine, et de aliis perfectionibus, quas homines ex superstitione et ignorantia perfectiones vocare voluerunt."]

LEMMA 2

The nature of a being which has the power to conserve itself
entails necessary existence.

Demonstration. Whoever has the power of conserving himself
has also the power of creating himself (by Axiom 10): that is
(as everyone will readily admit), he needs no external cause
for existence, his nature alone being the sufficient cause that
he exists, either possibly or necessarily. But not possibly, for
in that case (as I demonstrated in connection with Axiom 10)
it would not follow from the fact that he existed already that
he would exist hereafter (but this is against the hypothesis).
Therefore, such a being exists necessarily: that is, his nature
entails necessary existence.—Q.E.D.

Demonstration of Proposition VII. If I had the force to conserve myself, my nature would entail necessary existence (by
Lemma 2); therefore (by the Corollary of Lemma 1), my nature
would contain all perfections. But I find in myself as a thinking thing many imperfections (as that I doubt, that I desire,
and so forth), of which (by the Scholium to Proposition IV) I
am certain; therefore, I have no power to conserve myself. And
I cannot say that I lack these perfections because I now wish
to deny them to myself, for this would clearly be incompatible
with Lemma 1 and with what I clearly discover (by Axiom 5)
in myself.

Moreover, I cannot exist now without being conserved,
whether I exist through myself, if indeed I have the power, or
through another who has that power (by Axioms 10 and 11).
But I do exist (by the Scholium to Proposition IV), and yet
I do not have the power of conserving myself, as already has
been proved; therefore I am conserved by another. But not by
another who does not have the power of conserving himself
(by the same reason through which I just demonstrated that
I cannot conserve myself); therefore, by another whose nature

entails necessary existence, that is (by the Corollary of Lemma 1), by a being who contains all the perfections which I clearly understand to belong to a being entirely perfect. And, therefore, a being entirely perfect—that is (by Definition 8), God—exists, as was to be demonstrated.

COROLLARY

God can accomplish everything which we clearly perceive, just as we perceive it.

Demonstration.[13] All this clearly follows from the preceding proposition. For that God exists was proved there from the fact that someone [*aliquis*] must exist in whom there are all the perfections of which we possess any idea. But there is in us an idea of a power so great that heaven and earth, and everything else conceivably possible, could come into existence from him alone in whom that power exists. Therefore, in proving the existence of God we have proved at the same time all the things concerning him.

PROPOSITION VIII [14]

Mind and body are really distinct.

Demonstration. Whatever we clearly perceive can be accomplished by God just as we perceive it (by the preceding corollary). But we clearly perceive mind, that is (by Definition 6) thinking substance independent of body, that is (by Definition 7) independent of any extended substance (by Propositions III and IV), and, vice versa, we perceive body apart from mind (as everyone readily allows). Therefore, by divine power at least, mind can exist without body and body without mind.

Now, substances which can exist apart from one another are really distinct (by Definition 10); but mind and body are

13 [From Descartes, "Reply to Objections II," Prop. III, Corollary.]
14 [With this proposition Spinoza concludes his direct borrowings from Descartes' "Reply to the Second Set of Objections."]

substances (by Definitions 5, 6 and 7) which can exist apart
from one another (as was just proved); therefore mind and
body are really distinct.

See Proposition IV toward the end of Descartes' "Reply to
the Second Set of Objections," and the discussion in Part One
of the *Principles* from Principle 22 through Principle 29. For
I judge there is no need to describe these things here.

PROPOSITION IX

God is supremely intelligent.

Demonstration. If you deny it, then God either understands
nothing, or understands some things but not everything. But
to understand only some things and to be ignorant of the rest
supposes a limited and imperfect understanding, which can be
ascribed to God only with absurdity (by Definition 8). Yet
that God should understand nothing either indicates a lack
of understanding in him, as in men when they understand
nothing, and entails an imperfection which has no place in
God, or it indicates that God's understanding something is incompatible with his perfection. But when intelligence is thus
denied of God outright, he will be unable to create any intellect (by Axiom 8). Since, however, we clearly and distinctly
perceive intellect, God can be its cause (by the Corollary of
Proposition VII). Therefore, it is not true that God's understanding something is incompatible with his perfection. Consequently, he will be supremely intelligent.—Q.E.D.

SCHOLIUM

Even though it must be granted, as is demonstrated in Proposition XVI, that God is incorporeal, still this is not to be
understood as though all the perfections of extension must be
removed from him, but only so far as the nature and properties
of extension involve a certain imperfection. This is also true
of God's capacity for knowing, as everyone admits who wishes
to understand beyond the common run of philosophers, and

as will be explained more fully in our Appendix, Part Two, Chapter VII.

PROPOSITION X

Whatever perfection is discovered in God is from God.

Demonstration. If you deny the proposition, then suppose that there exists in God some perfection which is not from God. It will exist in God either from itself or from something distinct from God. If from itself, then it will possess necessary or at least possible existence (by Lemma 2 of Proposition VII), so that (by the Corollary of Lemma 1 of Proposition VII) it will be supremely perfect and consequently (by Definition 8) will be God. So to say that something exists in God from itself is the same as saying that it exists from God—Q.E.D. But if it exists from something distinct from God, then God cannot be conceived as utterly perfect per se, contrary to Definition Eight. Therefore, whatever perfection is discovered in God is from God.—Q.E.D.

PROPOSITION XI

There are not several Gods.

Demonstration. If you deny it, conceive, if possible, several Gods, *A* and *B*; then necessarily (by Proposition IX) both *A* and *B* will be supremely intelligent, so that *A* will understand everything, including himself and *B; B*, in turn, will understand himself and *A*. But since *A* and *B* exist necessarily (by Proposition V), the cause of the truth and necessity of the idea of *B*, which is in *A*, is *B* itself; and, on the other hand, the cause of the truth and necessity of the idea of *A*, which is in *B*, is *A* itself. On this account there will be a certain perfection in *A* which is not from *A*, and in *B* which is not from *B*, so that (by the preceding proposition) neither *A* nor *B* will be Gods. And so there are not several Gods.—Q.E.D.

Notice here how it necessarily follows simply from the fact

that a thing of itself entails necessary existence that the thing is unique, as is the case with God. Everyone could see this for himself with attentive study and I could have demonstrated it here in the same manner used in this proposition, but perhaps it would not have been perceptible to everyone.

PROPOSITION XII

Everything that exists is kept in existence [*conservatur*] solely by the power of God.

Demonstration. If you deny it, suppose that something keeps itself in existence; then (by Lemma 2 of Proposition VII) its nature entails necessary existence. Accordingly (by the Corollary of Lemma 1 of Proposition VII), it would be God and several Gods would exist, which is absurd (by the preceding proposition). Therefore, nothing exists which is not kept in existence solely by the power of God.—Q.E.D.

COROLLARY 1

God is the creator of all things.

Demonstration. God (by the preceding proposition) keeps everything in existence; that is (by Axiom 10), he has created and still continually creates everything that exists.

COROLLARY 2

Of themselves things have no essence which might be a cause of God's knowledge; on the contrary, God is the cause of things, including even their essence.

Demonstration. Since no perfection is found in God which is not from God (by Proposition X), things will of themselves have no essence which could be a cause of God's knowledge. On the contrary, since God has created all things outright and did not generate them out of something else (by Proposition

XII and its corollary), and since the act of creation reveals no other cause but the efficient (for so I define creation), which is God, it follows that before creation things were nothing and that accordingly God was also the cause of their essence.— Q.E.D.

Notice that this corollary is also evident from God's being the cause or the creator of all things (by the first corollary) and because a cause ought to contain in itself all the perfections of its effect (by Axiom 8), as everyone can readily see.

COROLLARY 3

Hence it clearly follows that God does not sense and does not, strictly speaking, perceive, for his understanding is not determined by anything outside himself; rather, all things flow from him.

COROLLARY 4

Through his causality God is prior to the essence and existence of things, as clearly follows from Corollaries 1 and 2 of this proposition.

PROPOSITION XIII

God is utterly truthful and not at all a deceiver.

Demonstration. We can attribute to God (by Definition 8) nothing in which we see any imperfection. And since every deception or intention to deceive proceeds (as is self-evident) [15]

15 I have not placed this axiom among the others, since there was no need; I did not need it except to demonstrate this proposition, and also, so long as I disregarded the existence of God, I was unwilling to assume anything as true except what I could deduce from the prime cognition, *ego sum,* as I noted in the Scholium to Proposition IV. Moreover, I did not place the definitions of fear and malice among the definitions, since no one is ignorant of them, and I did not need them except for this single proposition.

only from malice or fear, while fear supposes diminished strength and malice a privation of good, no deception or intention to deceive should be ascribed to God, a being utterly powerful and good; on the contrary, he must be called entirely truthful and not at all a deceiver.—Q.E.D. (See "Reply to the Second Set of Objections," Number 4.)

PROPOSITION XIV

Whatever we clearly and distinctly perceive is true.

Demonstration. The faculty of distinguishing true from false, which is in us (as everyone sees in himself and as can be seen from what we have already demonstrated), was created and is continually kept in existence by God (by Proposition XII and its corollaries); that is (by the preceding proposition), by a being utterly truthful and not at all a deceiver. And he has not given us any faculty (as everyone sees in himself) of abstaining or of not assenting to things which we clearly and distinctly perceive. Consequently, if we were deceived in these things, we would be deceived entirely by God and he would be a deceiver, but this (by the preceding proposition) is absurd. Accordingly, whatever we clearly and distinctly perceive is true.—Q.E.D.

SCHOLIUM

Since those things are necessarily true to which we must necessarily give our assent when we perceive them clearly and distinctly, and since we have a faculty of not assenting to what is obscure and dubious or cannot be deduced from certain principles, it clearly follows that we can always avoid falling into error and can avoid ever being deceived (this will be understood still more clearly from what follows), provided only that we seriously decide for ourselves to affirm nothing that we do not clearly and distinctly perceive or which has not been deduced from principles that are clear and certain in themselves.

PROPOSITION XV

Error is not something positive.

Demonstration. If error were something positive it would have God as its sole cause, by whom it would have to be continually created anew (by Proposition XII). But this is absurd (by Proposition XIII). Therefore, error is not something positive.— Q.E.D.

SCHOLIUM

Since error is not anything positive in man, it can only be a privation of the right use of freedom (by the Scholium to Proposition XIV); accordingly, God may be called the cause of error only in the sense in which we say that the absence of the sun is the cause of darkness, or in the sense in which God is called the cause of blindness in a child because he made it similar to others except in sight, for it is obvious that God gave us an intellect which extends only to a few things. To understand this clearly and, at the same time, to understand how error depends solely upon the misuse of our will, and finally how we can avoid error, let us recollect the modes of thinking we possess, which, obviously, are all the modes of perceiving (as sensing, imagining, and pure understanding) and the modes of willing (as desiring, refusing, affirming, denying, and doubting), for all can be referred to these two.

Concerning these we should notice first that mind, to the extent that it understands things clearly and distinctly and assents to them, cannot be mistaken (by Proposition XIV); neither can it be mistaken so long as it merely perceives things and does not assent to them. For even if at this moment I were perceiving a winged horse, it is certain that this perception would entail no falsehood so long as I do not assent, saying that it *is* a winged horse, nor even so long as I doubt whether the winged horse exists. And since to assent is simply to determine the will, error consequently depends solely upon a use of the will.

That this may appear more clearly, notice next that we have the power to assent not only to what we clearly and distinctly perceive, but also to what we perceive in any manner whatsoever.

For our will is not bound by limits. Anyone can see this clearly as soon as he considers that, should God wish to make our faculty of understanding infinite, he would not need to give us a more ample faculty of assent than the one we have to enable us to assent to all the things we would then understand. But the faculty we now possess would suffice for assenting to an infinity of things. In fact, we know by experience that we assent to many things which we have not deduced from known principles. From all this, moreover, it is perfectly clear that if the intellect should extend as far as the faculty of will, or if the faculty of will could extend no farther than intellect, or finally, if we could keep the faculty of will within the limits of the intellect, we could never fall into error (by Proposition XIV).

However, we lack the power to realize the first two conditions, for such a power implies that will should not be infinite and that intellect should not have been created finite. But the third condition remains to be considered: whether we have the power to keep our faculty of assent within the limits of the intellect. Now, since the will is free to determine itself, it follows that we have the power of keeping our faculty of assent within the limits of the intellect and, thus, of preventing our falling into error; whence, obviously, it depends solely on the use of free will never to be mistaken. That our will is free is demonstrated in *Principles,* Part One, Principle 39, and in the "Fourth Meditation," and we show it also at length in the last chapter of our Appendix. And if, when we perceive a thing clearly and distinctly, we cannot refuse to assent to it, this necessary assent depends only on the liberty and perfection of our will and not on its infirmity. For to assent is truly a perfection in us (as is evident enough in itself), and the will is never more perfect, nor more free, than when it directly determines itself. Because this can happen whenever the mind understands anything clearly and distinctly, it will endow itself immediately and necessarily with that perfection (by Axiom 5). We do not mean that since we are not indifferent when we embrace truth, we are less free. On the contrary, we have determined with certainty that the more indifferent we are, the less we are free.

So now there remains only to explain how error for men is mere privation, but for God is pure negation. We shall easily see this if we notice first that when we perceive more things than we clearly understand, we are more perfect than if we did not perceive them. This is clearly established by the following consideration: suppose that we could perceive nothing clearly and distinctly, but perceived all things confusedly; we would then possess no greater perfection than to perceive things confusedly, and nothing else could be desired for our nature. Besides, to the extent that assent even to confused things is an action, it is a perfection. This will also be manifest to anyone who supposes, as above, that it is repugnant to the nature of man to perceive things clearly and distinctly, for then, obviously, it will turn out to be far better for man to assent to things even if they are confused, and to exercise his freedom, than to remain permanently indifferent, that is (as we have just shown) to rest in the lowest grade of freedom. If we are also willing to regard the use and interest of human life, we will straightway discover that the exercise of will is absolutely necessary, as daily experience sufficiently teaches each of us.

Accordingly, since all the modes of thinking we possess, regarded solely in themselves, are perfect, whatever constitutes the form of error cannot exist in them considered simply in themselves. But if we examine the modes of willing, according as they differ from one another, we will find that some are more perfect than others in proportion as some make the will less indifferent and more free. Then we will also see that so long as we assent to confused things we make our minds less apt for distinguishing true from false, and thus cause ourselves to lack the optimum freedom. Consequently, assent to confused things, to the extent that such assent is something positive, does not contain imperfection nor the form of error, but it does contain imperfection to the extent that we deprive ourselves of that optimum freedom which belongs to our nature and is in our power. Accordingly, the entire imperfection of error consists solely in the privation of complete freedom, and this privation is called error. It is called a privation because we are deprived of a perfection which pertains to our nature; it is called error because we lack that perfection through our own fault, by not keeping the will within the limits of the understanding as much as we can. Since, then, for man error is nothing but the privation of a perfect and right use of freedom, it follows that it is not located in any faculty which man has from God, nor in any exercise of these faculties so far as that exercise depends on God. Similarly, we cannot say that God has deprived us of a stronger intellect which he could have given us, and thus made us able to fall into errors. For the nature of a thing cannot demand anything of God, and nothing belongs to anything beyond what the will of God has willed to grant it, for nothing existed and nothing can be conceived prior to the will of God (as will be more fully explained in Part Two, Chapters VII and VIII of our Appendix). Therefore, God has no more deprived us of a stronger intellect or more perfect faculty of understanding than he has deprived a circle of the properties of a globe, or a circumference of the properties of a sphere.

Since, then, none of our faculties, however considered, can reveal an imperfection in God, it clearly follows that the imperfection in which the form of error consists is, in respect of men, mere privation; but in relation to God as its cause it can only be called negation, and not privation.

PROPOSITION XVI

God is incorporeal.

Demonstration. Body is the immediate subject of local motion (by Definition 7); therefore, if God were corporeal, he would be divided into parts; but since this clearly involves imperfection, it is absurd (by Definition 8) to affirm it of God.

Another Demonstration. If God were corporeal, he could be divided into parts (by Definition 7). In this event, each part of God could either subsist by itself or it could not. If the latter, it would be similar to all the other things created by God, and, consequently, like every created thing would continually be created anew by God through the same force (by Proposition X and Axiom 11), and would no more belong to the nature of God than all other created things; but this is absurd (by Proposition V). However, if each part of God exists through itself, each part must also entail necessary existence (by Lemma 2 of Proposition VII), and consequently each part would be an utterly perfect being (by the Corollary of Lemma 2 of Proposition VII). But this also is absurd (by Proposition XI); therefore God is incorporeal.—Q.E.D.

PROPOSITION XVII

God is a being utterly simple.

Demonstration. If God were composed of parts, the parts (as everyone will readily allow) must be prior to God, at least in their nature, which is absurd (by Corollary 4 of Proposition XII). Accordingly, he is a being utterly simple.—Q.E.D.

COROLLARY

Hence it follows that the understanding of God, and his will —that is, his decree and power—are not distinct from his essence except in reason.

PROPOSITION XVIII

God is immutable.

Demonstration. If God were mutable, he could not be changed in part, but would have to be altered in his entire essence (by

Proposition XVII). But the essence of God exists necessarily (by Propositions V, VI, and VII). Therefore, God is immutable.—Q.E.D.

PROPOSITION XIX

God is eternal.

Demonstration. God is a being supremely perfect (by Definition 8), and so (by Proposition V) he exists necessarily. If now we attribute a limited existence to him, necessarily the limits of his existence must be understood, at least by God himself, if not by us (by Proposition IX), since he is supremely intelligent. Consequently, God, a being utterly perfect (by Definition 8), would understand that he does not exist beyond these limits, which is absurd (by Proposition V). Therefore, God has an infinite existence which we call eternity, and not a limited existence. (See Part Two, Chapter I of our Appendix.) Accordingly, God is eternal.—Q.E.D.

PROPOSITION XX

God has preordained all things from eternity.

Demonstration. Since God is eternal (by the preceding proposition), his knowledge will be eternal since it pertains to his eternal essence (by the Corollary of Proposition XVII). Therefore, to say that God has understood things from eternity is the same as saying that he has willed or decreed things so from eternity.—Q.E.D.

COROLLARY

From this proposition it follows that God is entirely constant in his works.

PROPOSITION XXI

Substance extended in length, breadth, and depth truly exists; and we are united to one part of it.

Demonstration. Extended matter, as we clearly and distinctly perceive it, does not pertain to God (by Proposition X). But it can be created by God (by the Corollary of Proposition VII and by Proposition VIII). Now we clearly and distinctly perceive (as everyone, to the extent that he thinks, discovers in himself) that extended substance is a cause sufficient to produce in us pleasurable excitement, grief, and similar ideas or sensations which are continually produced in us, even against our wills. But if we try to fashion a cause of sensations other than extended substance, say God or an angel, we at once destroy this clear and distinct concept we have. For this reason,[16] so long as we rightly attend to our own perceptions and admit nothing save what we clearly and distinctly perceive, we will not be indifferent, but will have a tendency to affirm that extended substance is the sole cause of our sensations, and, thus, to affirm that extended matter, created by God, exists. In affirming this we certainly cannot be deceived (by Proposition XIV and its Scholium). Therefore, it is truly affirmed that substance, extended in length, breadth, and depth, exists. This was our first point.

Moreover, among the sensations which (as we have now demonstrated) must be produced in us by extended substance, we notice a great difference, for example, the difference between saying that I sense or see a tree, or saying that I am thirsty or grieved, and so forth. Yet I clearly see that I am not able to perceive the cause of this difference unless I first understand that I am closely united to one part of matter, but not to others. But since I do clearly and distinctly understand this and could not perceive it in any other way, it is true (by Proposition XIV and its Scholium) that I am united to one part of matter. This was our second point. Therefore, we have demonstrated what was to be demonstrated.

Note: Unless the reader regards himself here only as a thinking thing, lacking a body, and sets aside as prejudices all the reasons he has held heretofore for believing that body exists, it will be useless for him to try to understand this demonstration.

[16] See Demonstration of Prop. XIV, and Scholium to Prop. XV.

PART TWO

POSTULATE

We ask here only that everyone attend as accurately as possible to his own perceptions so he can distinguish the clear from the obscure.

DEFINITIONS

1. *Extension* is that which consists of three dimensions; by extension, however, we do not mean the act of extending, nor anything different from quantity.

2. By *substance* we mean that which needs only the concursus of God to exist.

3. An *atom* is a part of matter by its very nature indivisible.

4. The *indefinite* is that whose limits (if it has any) cannot be searched out by human intellect.

5. A *vacuum* is extension without corporeal substance.

6. We distinguish *space* from extension only in reason; actually there is no difference. (Read *Principles,* Part II, Principle 10.)

7. What we know to be divided by thought is *divisible,* at least potentially.

8. *Local motion* is the transfer of one part of matter or of one body from the vicinity of those bodies immediately touching it, which are regarded as at rest, into the vicinity of others.

Descartes uses this definition to explain local motion. To understand it rightly we must consider:

a) That he means by a part of matter everything which is transferred at one time, even if it can consist of many parts.

b) That to avoid confusion in this definition he mentions only what constantly exists in a mobile thing, namely, its transfer, to prevent its being confused, as has happened with others in

53

various places, with the force or action that does the moving. This force or action, it is generally believed, is required only for motion and not for rest, but this belief is plainly wrong. For it is self-evident that the same force is required to impress several degrees of motion upon a body instantaneously as is required to remove these degrees of motion from that body all at once, so that it is completely at rest. But this can also be proved from experience. For we use very nearly an equal force in propelling a boat at rest in stagnant water as we do in stopping it suddenly, once it is moved; actually, the force would be exactly the same if we were not helped to stop it by the weight and sluggishness of the water displaced by the boat.

c) That he says transfer takes place from the vicinity of contiguous bodies into the vicinity of others, and not from one place to another. For place (as he himself explained in *Principles,* Part II, Principle 13) is not something actual, but depends only on our thought; so much so that the same body can be said to change and not change its place at the same time; but it cannot be said to be transferred and not transferred at the same time from the vicinity of a contiguous body, since only single bodies can at the same instant be contiguous to the same mobile body.

d) That he does not assert absolutely that transfer takes place from the vicinity of adjoining bodies, but only from the vicinity of those which are regarded as at rest. For to transfer a body *A* from body *B* which is at rest, the same force and action are required from one side as from the other. This is clearly the case with a skiff, for example, sticking to the mud or sand at the bottom of the water, since to propel the skiff an

equal force must necessarily be impressed upon the water's bottom and upon the boat. For this reason, the force by which bodies must be moved is applied equally to the body moved and to the one at rest. Transfer is really reciprocal: if the skiff is separated from the sand, the sand in turn is separated from the skiff. If, then, we should want to attribute absolutely equal motions to bodies which are separated from one another, each in a different direction, and not regard one of them as at rest simply because the action in the one is the same as in the other, we would also be compelled to attribute to bodies which everyone regards as at rest—for example, to the sand from which the skiff is separated—as much motion as is attributed to bodies that are moved, since, as we have shown, the same action is required by the one as by the other and transfer is reciprocal. But this is far removed from the common use of speech. Nevertheless, although these bodies from which the others are separated are regarded and spoken of as at rest, still we will recollect that everything in a moved body, through which it is said to be moved, is also in a quiescent body.

e) Finally, from the definition it is also clearly apparent that each body has precisely one motion proper to itself, since it is understood to recede only from single bodies contiguous to it and at rest. Still, if the moved body is part of other bodies possessing other motion, we clearly see that it too can share in innumerable other motions. But since a great many motions cannot be easily perceived at one time and indeed since all of them cannot be distinguished, it is enough to consider in itself that unique motion proper to each body. (Read *Principles,* Part II, Principle 31.)

9. By *a circle of moved bodies* we only mean the situation in which the last body, moved through the impulse of another

body, immediately touches the first of the moved bodies, however contorted be the line which will be described by all the bodies instantaneously through the impulse of a single motion.

AXIOMS

1. "Nothing" has no properties.

2. Whatever can be taken away from a thing while the thing remains unchanged does not constitute its essence; but that which destroys the thing, if it is removed, does constitute its essence.

3. In "hardness," sense indicates to us, and we clearly and

distinctly understand from it, nothing more than that the parts of hard bodies resist the motion of our hands.

4. If two bodies recede from or approach one another, they will not on that account occupy more or less space.

5. Whether a part of matter gives way or resists, it does not for that reason lose the nature of body.

6. Motion, rest, figure, and the like cannot be conceived without extension.

7. Apart from sensible qualities there is nothing in a body but extension and the affections which are listed in Part One of the *Principles*.

8. One space, or a particular extension, cannot be larger at one time than at another.

9. Every extension can be divided, at least in thought.

No one who is at all acquainted with the elements of mathematics can doubt the truth of this axiom. For the space between a circle and a tangent can always be divided by an infinity of larger circles. This is also evident in the asymptotes of a hyperbola.

10. No one can conceive the limits of a particular extension or space, unless at the same time he conceives, beyond these limits, other spaces immediately contiguous to the first.

11. If matter is multiple and if one matter does not immediately touch another, each necessarily will be contained within limits beyond which no matter exists.

12. Extremely minute bodies easily give way to the motion of our hands.

13. One space does not penetrate another space, and is not larger at one time than at another.

14. If a pipe *A* is of the same length as pipe *C*, while *C* is twice as broad as *A*, and if some fluid material flows through *A* twice as quickly as that which passes through *C*, then in the same time the same amount of material will flow through *A* as through *C*. And if the same amount flows through pipe *A* as through *C*, it will be moved twice as quickly through *A*.

15. Things which agree with the same third thing agree with one another. Also, things which are double the same third thing are equal to one another.

16. Matter moved in different ways has at least as many parts, actually divided, as the various degrees of speed observed in it at one time.

17. The shortest line between two points is a straight line.

18. If body *A* which is moved from *C* toward *B* is repelled by an opposite impulse, it will be moved toward *C* along the same line.

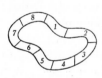

19. When bodies having opposite motions meet one another, both, or at least one, are compelled to suffer some variation.

20. Variation in a thing comes from a stronger force.

21. If, when body *1* is moved toward body *2* and drives it along, body *8* also is moved through this impulse toward *1*, then bodies *1, 2, 3*, and so forth, cannot exist in a straight line; instead, all of them complete a whole circle back to body *1*. (See Part II, Definition 9.)

LEMMA 1

Where there is extension or space there is necessarily substance.

Demonstration. Extension or space cannot (by Axiom 1, Part II) be pure nothing; it is, therefore, an attribute which must necessarily be attributed to something. Not to God, however (by Proposition XVI, Part I); consequently, to a thing which needs nothing but the concursus of God to exist (by Proposition XII, Part I); that is, to substance (by Definition 2, Part II).—Q.E.D.

LEMMA 2

Rarefaction and condensation are clearly and distinctly conceived, but we do not concede that bodies when rarefied occupy more space than when condensed.

Demonstration. Rarefaction and condensation can be clearly and distinctly conceived through the simple fact that the parts of a particular body withdraw from one another or approach one another. Consequently (by Axiom 4 in Part II), they will occupy neither a larger nor a smaller space. For if the parts of a body, say a sponge, through approaching one another expel the bodies with which the intervening spaces are filled, the body will only be made more dense, and the parts will not on that account occupy less space than before (by Axiom 4 in Part II). If, on the other hand, they recede from one another and the intervening passages become filled with other bodies, rarefaction will result, and still the parts will not occupy a larger space. This phenomenon, which with the help of our senses we see clearly in a sponge, we can conceive in all bodies through the intellect alone, even though the intervening spaces escape human sense. Thus, we conceive rarefaction and condensation clearly and distinctly.—Q.E.D.

It seemed proper to make these preliminary remarks, in order to free the intellect of its prejudices about space, rarefaction, and so forth, and to make it apt for understanding the things that follow.

PROPOSITION I

Even if hardness, weight, and the other sensible qualities are separated from a body, its bodily nature will remain unimpaired.

Demonstration. In the hardness, say, of a stone, sense indicates to us, and we clearly and distinctly understand from it, nothing more than that the parts of hard bodies resist the motion of our hands (by Axiom 3, Part II). Hardness, consequently (by Proposition XIV, Part I), will be nothing more than this. If, in fact, this body is reduced to the finest possible dust, its parts will easily recede (by Axiom 12, Part II), and yet will not lose the nature of body (by Axiom 5, Part II).—Q.E.D.

The demonstration with respect to weight and the other sensible qualities proceeds in the same way.

PROPOSITION II

The nature of body or matter consists solely in extension.

Demonstration. The nature of body is not destroyed with the removal of the sensible qualities (by Proposition I, Part II); consequently, the sensible qualities do not constitute its essence (by Axiom 2, Part II). Nothing remains, therefore, but extension and its affection (by Axiom 7, Part II). Thus, if extension is taken away, nothing having the nature of body will remain, and corporeal nature will be taken away completely; therefore (by Axiom 2, Part II), the nature of body consists solely in extension.—Q.E.D.

COROLLARY

Space and body are not actually different.

Demonstration. Body and extension are not actually different (by the preceding proposition); nor are space and extension actually different (by Definition 6, Part II); therefore (by Axiom 15, Part II), space and body are not actually different.—Q.E.D.

SCHOLIUM

Although we say that God is everywhere,[1] we do not thereby concede that God is extended, that is (by the preceding proposition), that he is corporeal. For to be everywhere refers solely to God's power and to the concursus by which he conserves all things: so much so, that God's ubiquity may no more be referred to extension or to body than to angels and human souls. But notice that when we say God's power is everywhere, we do not separate it from his essence; for where his power is, there his essence is also (by the Corollary of Proposition XVII, Part I). Rather, we only set his power apart from corporeity; that

[1] See more fully concerning this in the Appendix, Part II, Chaps. III and IX.

is, God is everywhere, not through any corporeal power, but through the divine power or essence which extends equally to the conservation of extension and to that of thinking beings (by Proposition XVII, Part I). In fact, he could not conserve thinking beings if his power or essence were corporeal.

PROPOSITION III

It is inconsistent to say that a vacuum exists.

Demonstration. By a vacuum is meant extension without corporeal substance (by Definition 5, Part II); that is (by Proposition II, Part II), a vacuum is body without body, which is absurd.

For a fuller explanation and to correct any prejudice regarding vacuums, read Principles 17 and 18 of Part Two of the *Principles,* where it is expressly shown that when nothing intervenes between bodies, they necessarily touch one another, and also that "nothing" has no properties.

PROPOSITION IV

One part of body does not occupy more space at one time than at another, and, conversely, the same space does not contain more body at one time than at another.

Demonstration. Space and body are not actually different (by the Corollary to Proposition II, Part II). Therefore, when we say that space is not larger at one time than at another (by Axiom 13, Part II), we are saying that body cannot be larger, or occupy a larger space, at one time than at another. This was the first point. Then from the fact that space and body are not actually different, when we say body cannot occupy more space at one time than at another, it follows that we are saying that the same space cannot contain more body at one time than at another.—Q.E.D.

COROLLARY

Bodies which occupy an equal space, gold and air for instance, possess an equal amount of matter or corporeal substance.

Demonstration. Corporeal substance does not consist of hardness, as in gold, nor of softness, as in air, nor of any of the sensible qualities (by Proposition I, Part II), but solely in extension (by Proposition II, Part II). But since (by hypothesis) there is as much space, or (by Definition 6, Part II) extension, in the one as in the other, therefore there will also be as much corporeal substance.—Q.E.D.

PROPOSITION V

There are no atoms.

Demonstration. Atoms are parts of matter by their very nature indivisible (by Definition 3, Part II). But since the nature of matter consists in extension (by Proposition II, Part II), which however small is by its very nature divisible (by Axiom 9 and Definition 7, Part II), therefore a part of matter however small is by its nature divisible: that is, there are no atoms or parts of matter by their very nature indivisible.—Q.E.D.

SCHOLIUM

The question about atoms has always been difficult and intricate. Some have claimed that atoms exist for the reason that one infinity cannot be greater than another infinity. Now, if two quantities, say A and a quantity twice as great, were infinitely divisible, they could through the power of God, who sees in one glance their infinite parts, be actually divided into infinite parts. Therefore since, as was said, one infinity is not greater than another, the quantity A will be equal to the quantity twice as great, which is absurd. They also ask whether half of an infinite number is also infinite, and whether it is equal or unequal, and other such questions. To all these Descartes replied that we should not reject things which fall within the grasp of our intellect and which consequently are clearly and distinctly conceived because of other things which exceed our intellect or grasp and which are for that reason perceived only inadequately. But the infinite and its properties do exceed the human intellect, which is by nature finite; consequently it would be inept to reject as false, or to doubt, what we conceive clearly and distinctly about space on the grounds that we do not comprehend the infinite. This is why Descartes takes as indefinite things in which we see no limits, such as the extension of the universe, the divisibility of the parts of matter, and the like. (See *Principles,* Part I, Principle 26.)

PROPOSITION VI

Matter is indefinitely extended; and is one and the same in the heavens or on earth.

Demonstration of the First Part. We cannot imagine any limits to extension, that is (by Proposition II, Part II), to matter, without conceiving beyond these limits other spaces immediately contiguous (by Axiom 10, Part II); that is (by Definition 6, Part II), we would conceive extension or matter, and would conceive it indefinitely. This was the first point.

Demonstration of the Second Part. The essence of matter consists in extension (by Proposition II, Part II), and this is indefinite (by the first part of this demonstration), that is (by Definition 4, Part II), such as cannot be conceived by the human intellect under any limits; therefore (by Axiom 11, Part II), matter is not multiple, but is everywhere one and the same. This was the second point.

SCHOLIUM

Thus far we have considered the nature or essence of extension. Moreover, in the last proposition of Part One we demonstrated that extension, created by God, exists just as we conceive it; and from Proposition XII of Part One it follows that extension is now conserved by the same force through which it was created. We also demonstrated in the last proposition of Part I that we ourselves, as thinking beings, are united to a particular part of this matter. By means of this part of matter, we perceive the actual existence of all those variations of which, solely through reflection on matter, we know matter is capable: such variations as divisibility, local motion, or the migration of one part from one place to another, as we clearly and distinctly perceive as soon as we understand that other parts of matter take the place of those which are displaced. Moreover, this division and motion in matter are conceived in infinite ways, and, consequently, infinite variations can be conceived in matter. I say that we conceive these variations clearly and distinctly, so long as we conceive them as modes of extension and not as things really distinct from extension, as was fully explained in Part I of the *Principles*. Although philosophers have imagined many other kinds of motion, we, who will admit only what we clearly and distinctly conceive, must allow nothing but local motion, because we clearly and distinctly understand that extension is not capable of any motion but local motion, and that, moreover, no other motion falls within the grasp of our imagination.

Zeno, of course, is said to have denied local motion for various reasons. Diogenes the Cynic, walking through the school where these doctrines were being taught by Zeno, refuted them in his own way by disturbing Zeno's students as he walked. When he felt himself blocked by a student who sought to prevent his passage, he chided him, saying, "Why do you dare thus to refute the arguments of your master?" However, lest anyone, deceived by Zeno's arguments, think that the senses make known to us anything—in particular, any motion—clearly inconsistent with intellect, so that the mind itself, through the work of the intellect, may be deceived regarding things it clearly and distinctly perceives, I shall list here Zeno's principal arguments and show that they depend entirely upon false prejudices, which is not surprising since he had no true concept of matter.

First, he is said to have held that if local motion were to exist, then the motion of a body moved circularly as rapidly as possible would not differ from rest; but the consequent is absurd; therefore, the hypothesis also. He proves the consequent as follows: A body is at rest when all of its points remain constantly in the same place; but all the points of a body moved circularly as rapidly as possible remain constantly in the same place; therefore, etc. He is said to have explained this by the example of a wheel, say *ABC*. If this wheel is moved about its center at a certain speed, the point *A* will complete

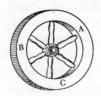

the circle through *B* and *C* more quickly than if the wheel were moved more slowly. Suppose, for example, that the wheel is moved slowly, and that after the lapse of an hour point *A* is in the same place from which it began. If, then, the wheel is moved twice as quickly, point *A* will be in the place from which it began to move after the lapse of half an hour; if it is moved four times as quickly, after the lapse of fifteen minutes; and if we conceive the speed increased to infinity while the time is diminished to instants, then with the very greatest possible speed point *A* will constantly and at every instant be in the place from which it began to be moved, and so it always remains in the same place. Now what we understand here of point *A* must also be understood of every point on this wheel; consequently, at this maximum speed all the points remain constantly in the same place.

But notice, I reply, that this is more an argument against an absolute speed of motion than against motion itself. Whether Zeno argues correctly we shall not examine here; instead, we will reveal the prejudices upon which his whole reasoning depends, so far as it is thought to impugn motion. First, he supposes that bodies can be conceived to be moved so quickly that they cannot be moved faster. Second, he supposes that time is composed of instants, just as others have thought that quantity is composed of indivisible points. Both assumptions are false; for we can never conceive a motion so fast that we may not conceive at the same time another still faster. It is repugnant to our understanding to conceive a motion, however small the line it describes, so fast that a faster cannot exist. This objection also applies to slowness; for the supposition implies conceiving a motion so slow that a slower could not exist. We make the same objection with regard to time which is the measure of motion, namely, that it is inconsistent with thought to conceive a time so brief that one still briefer cannot exist. To prove all these objections, let us follow in Zeno's steps. Let us suppose then, as he did, that a wheel *ABC* is moved about its center with such a speed that point *A* is at every moment in the place *A* from which it is moved. I claim that I can clearly conceive a speed indefinitely more swift than this, and, consequently, instants infinitely smaller. For suppose that while the wheel *ABC* is moved about its center, it causes by means of a rope *H* another wheel *DEF* (half as large as the first) to

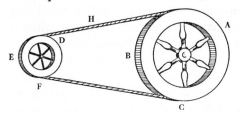

be moved about its center. Since we suppose wheel *DEF* to be half as large as wheel *ABC*, it is obvious that the wheel *DEF* is moved twice as quickly as the wheel *ABC*, and that, consequently, point *D* at each half instant is always in the same place from which it began to be moved. If then we attribute to wheel *ABC* the motion of wheel *DEF*, *DEF* in turn will be moved four times as quickly as before; and again, if we attribute this last speed of wheel *DEF* to wheel *ABC*, *DEF* will be moved eight times as quickly, and so ad infinitum. But this is already perfectly clear from the very concept of matter. For the essence of matter consists in extension or space, which, as we have proved, is always divisible; and there is no motion without space. We have also demonstrated that one part of matter cannot at the same time occupy two spaces, since this would be the same as saying that one part of matter is equal to its own double, as appears from our previous demonstrations. Therefore, if a part of matter is moved, it is moved through some particular space, and this space, however small it is imagined to be, will still be divisible, and consequently, also the time by which it is measured; and as a further consequence, the duration or time of this motion will be divisible, and so ad infinitum.— Q.E.D.

Let us proceed to another sophism, which he is said to have presented in the following form. If a body is moved, it is moved either in the place in which it is or in which it is not. But not where it is, for if it is in any place it is necessarily at rest. But not where it is not. Therefore, body is not moved. However, this reasoning is entirely like the preceding, for it supposes that there is a time in relation to which no shorter time exists. For if we should reply that a body is moved not in a place, but from the place in which it is to a place in which it is not, he will ask whether it was not in the intermediate places. We would reply with the distinction: if by *was* is meant *was at rest,* we deny that it was anywhere while it was being moved; but if by *was* is meant *existed,* we claim that while it was being moved it necessarily existed. Then he will ask where it existed while it was being moved. We would reply in turn: if by the words *where it existed* he means to ask *what place it remained in* while it was being moved, we claim that it remained in no place; but if he means *what place it moved from,* then we claim that it moved from all the places he cares to assign to the space through which it was moved. He will then ask whether it could both occupy and move from a place at the same instant. To this, finally, we reply with the following distinction: if by an instant he means a time in relation to which a shorter time cannot exist, his question is unintelligible, as has been sufficiently shown, and consequently unworthy of answer; but if he takes time in the sense which I explained above, which is its true sense, then no particle of time, however indefinitely brief it is imagined, can ever be postulated in which a body cannot both occupy and move from a place. This is sufficiently evident to anyone who gives it his attention. Clearly then, as we said before, Zeno supposes a time so brief that no shorter time can exist, and thus he proves nothing.

In addition to these two arguments, still another of Zeno's is commonly brought forward, which can be read along with its refutation in the next to last letter of the first volume of Descartes' *Epistles*.

Here I should like my readers to notice that I have opposed Zeno's reasons with my own, and thus have refuted him by reason rather than by sense as Diogenes did. For the senses cannot furnish to an investigator any truth other than the phenomena of nature, by which he is bound while investigating their causes; and the senses can never show anything to be false which the intellect clearly and distinctly apprehends as true. At least we think so, and, consequently, this is our method: to demonstrate the things which we propose, by means of reasons clearly and distinctly perceived by the intellect, and to keep our reasons intact whatever the senses dictate to the contrary. For the senses, as we have said, can only determine the intellect to investigate this rather than that and cannot charge it with error when it perceives anything clearly and distinctly.

PROPOSITION VII

No body enters into the place of another body unless that other body enters into the place of still another body.

Demonstration. (See the figure in the following proposition.) If you deny the proposition, assume, if it can be done, that a body A enters into the place of a body B, which I suppose is equal to A and does not recede from its own place. Thus the space which contained only B now contains (by hypothesis) both A and B, and consequently twice as much corporeal substance as formerly. This (by Proposition IV, Part II) is absurd. Therefore, no body enters into the place of another, and so forth.—Q.E.D.

PROPOSITION VIII

When a particular body enters into the place of another, the place deserted by it is at the same instant occupied by yet another body immediately contiguous to it.

Demonstration. If body *B* is moved toward *D,* bodies *A* and *C* at the same instant either approach one another and touch, or they do not. If they approach one another and touch, our proposition is granted. If, however, they do not approach one another, and the whole space deserted by *B* intervenes between *A* and *C,* then a body equal to *B* (by the Corollary of Proposition II and the Corollary of Proposition IV, Part II) lies between them. But this body is not (by hypothesis) *B;* therefore, it is another body which at the same instant moves into *B*'s place; and since it enters at the same instant, there can be no other result than that it be immediately contiguous to *B* (by the Scholium to Proposition VI, Part II); for in that scholium we demonstrated that no motion from one place into another exists which does not require an amount of time in relation to which a shorter time always exists. Consequently, the space of body *B* cannot at the same instant be occupied by a body which would have to be moved through some space before it entered into *B*'s place. Therefore, only a body immediately contiguous to *B* enters at the same instant into its place.—Q.E.D.

SCHOLIUM

Since the parts of matter are really distinct from one another (by Principle 61, Part I of the *Principles*), one can exist apart from another (by the Corollary of Proposition VII, Part I) and they do not depend upon one another. This is why all those fictions about sympathy and antipathy must be rejected as false. Moreover, since the cause of a given effect ought always to be something positive (by Axiom 8, Part I), it should never be said that a particular body is moved in order to avoid a vacuum, but only that it is moved through the impulse of another body.

COROLLARY

In every motion an entire circle of bodies is moved at one time.

Demonstration. At the time in which body *1* enters the place of body *2*, this body *2* should move into the place of another body, say *3*, and so on (by Proposition VII, Part II). Then at

the same instant in which body *1* enters the place of body *2*, the place deserted by body *1* ought to be filled by another body (by Proposition VIII, Part II), say body *8* or any other body immediately contiguous to

body *1*. Since this happens solely through the impulse of another body (by the preceding scholium), which in this case is supposed to be body *1*, all these bodies cannot be moved in the same straight line (by Axiom 21, Part II), but (by Definition 9, Part II) describe a complete circle.—Q.E.D.

PROPOSITION IX

If a circular pipe *ABC* is full of water and is four times as broad at point *A* as at point *B*, when the water (or any other fluid body) at point *A* begins to be moved toward point *B*, the water at *B* will be moved four times more quickly than the water at *A*.

Demonstration. Since all the water at point *A* is moved toward *B*, an equal amount of water should at the same time

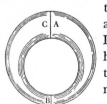

take its place from point *C*, which is immediately contiguous to *A* (by Proposition VIII, Part II); and an equal amount of water will have to enter the place *C* from point *B* (by the same proposition). Therefore, it will be moved four times as rapidly.—Q.E.D.

What we say here of a circular pipe should be understood of all unequal spaces through which bodies moved at the same time are compelled to pass, since the demonstration will be the same in all other cases.

If two semicircles are described about the same center, as in
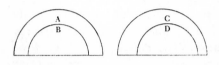
A and B, the space between their peripheries will be everywhere equal. But if they are described about different centers, as in C and D, the space between their peripheries will be everywhere unequal. The demonstration is obvious simply from the definition of a circle.

PROPOSITION X

A fluid body moved through pipe *ABC* admits indefinite degrees of speed.

Demonstration. (See the figure in the preceding proposition.) The space between A and B is everywhere unequal (by the preceding lemma): therefore (by Proposition IX, Part II), the speed with which a fluid body is moved through pipe *ABC* will be everywhere unequal. Moreover, since we may in thought conceive between A and B an indefinite number of spaces continually smaller (by Proposition V, Part II), we also conceive these inequalities which are everywhere present as indefinite, and so (by Proposition IX, Part II) their degrees of speed will be indefinite.—Q.E.D.

PROPOSITION XI

In the matter which flows through pipe *ABC,* there is a division into particles indefinite in number.

Demonstration. See the figure in Proposition IX.) The matter which flows through pipe *ABC* acquires simultaneously indefi-

nite degrees of speed (by Proposition X, Part II); therefore
(by Axiom 16, Part II), it possesses an indefinite number of
parts actually divided.—Q.E.D. (Read *Principles,* Part II, Principles 34 and 35.)

Thus far we have considered the nature of motion; now we
must consider its cause, which is twofold: its basic or gen-
eric cause, which is the cause of all motions in the universe,
and its particular cause, through which the single parts of
matter acquire the motions they did not previously have. In
regard to the general cause, since nothing is to be admitted
(by Proposition XIV and the Scholium to Proposition XVII,
Part I) unless we clearly and distinctly perceive it, and since
we clearly and distinctly understand no cause other than God
(the creator of matter), obviously no other general cause is
to be admitted but God. What is said here of motion is to be
understood of rest also.

PROPOSITION XII

God is the principal cause of motion.

Demonstration. Examine the scholium immediately preceding.

PROPOSITION XIII

God conserves now through his concursus the same quantity
of motion and rest which he first impressed upon matter.

Demonstration. Since God is the cause of motion and rest (by
Proposition XII, Part II), he conserves them still by the same
power through which he created them (by Axiom 10, Part I);
and indeed, in the same quantity in which he first created
them (by the Corollary of Proposition XX, Part I).—Q.E.D.

I. Although it is said in theology that God does many things according to his own good pleasure and in order to demonstrate his power to man, still, since the things that depend solely upon his pleasure come to be known only through divine revelation, they should not be admitted in philosophy, where investigation is directed only upon that which reason dictates. Otherwise, philosophy will be confounded with theology.

II. Although motion is nothing in the matter moved but a mode of this matter, it has nevertheless a specific and determinate quantity. How this comes to be known will appear below. (Read *Principles*, Part II, Principle 36.)

PROPOSITION XIV

Each particular thing, so far as it is simple and undivided, and is considered simply in itself, always perseveres as much as it can in the same state.

This proposition is regarded by many as axiomatic; however, we will demonstrate it.

Demonstration. Since nothing exists in any state save through the concursus of God (by Proposition XII, Part I), and since God is utterly constant in his own works (by the Corollary of Proposition XX, Part I), if we give our attention to no external causes—that is, to no particular causes—but consider the thing simply in itself, it will have to be admitted that the thing always perseveres as much as it can in the state in which it exists.—Q.E.D.

Once a body is moved it always continues to be moved, unless it is retarded by external causes.

Demonstration. This is obvious from the preceding proposition. However, to correct any prejudices about motion, read *Principles,* Part II, Principles 37 and 38.

PROPOSITION XV

Every body that is moved tends of itself to continue to be moved in a straight line rather than a curved.

This proposition might have been included in the axioms, but I will demonstrate it from what we have already said, as follows:

Demonstration. Motion, since it has only God as its cause (by Proposition XII, Part II), never possesses of itself any power to exist (by Axiom 10, Part I), but is, as it were, procreated [*procreatur*] by God at every instant (by what was said in the demonstration of Axiom 10, Part I). For this reason, so long as we consider only the nature of motion, we can never attribute to it as part of its nature a duration which can be thought of as greater than another. But should it be claimed as part of the nature of a moved body that the body describes a curved line through its motion, then a more lasting duration would be attributed to the nature of motion than would be attributed on the assumption that a moved body by nature tends to continue to be moved in a straight line (by Axiom 17, Part II). Since, however (as we have already demonstrated), we cannot attribute such a duration to the nature of motion, neither can we propose that it is of the nature of a moved body to be moved in a curved line, but only that it continues to be moved in a straight line.—Q.E.D.

SCHOLIUM

For many, perhaps, this demonstration will not seem to show sufficiently that it is not part of the nature of motion to describe a curved line rather than a straight line, since no straight line can be postulated in relation to which a smaller line, whether curved or straight, cannot exist, and since no curved line exists but that another, smaller curve exists also. Although I have these considerations in mind, still I think the demonstration proceeds correctly, seeing that it concludes what was proposed for demonstration solely from the universal essence or from the essential difference of the lines (and not from the quantity of a particular line or from an accidental difference). However, to avoid making a thing which is sufficiently clear in itself somewhat obscure by demonstrating it, I call the reader's attention to the definition of motion, which affirms nothing of motion but the transfer of one part of matter from the vicinity, etc., to the vicinity of others, etc. Consequently, unless we conceive this transfer to be as simple as possible, that is, to occur along a straight line, we add something to motion which is not contained in its definition or essence, and which accordingly does not belong to its nature.

COROLLARY

It follows from this proposition that every body which is moved along a curved line continually turns aside from the line along which it would, of itself, continue to be moved, and this happens through the force of some external cause (by Proposition XIV, Part II).

PROPOSITION XVI

Every body that is moved in a circle, as, for example, a stone in a sling, is continually determined to continue its motion along a tangent.

Demonstration. A body that is moved in a circle is continually impeded by an external force from continuing its motion along a straight line (by the Corollary of the preceding proposition); when the external force ceases, the body continues of itself to be moved along a straight line (by Proposition XV, Part II). Now I claim that a body which is moved in a circle is determined by an external cause to continue its motion along a tangent. If you deny the proposition, let it be supposed that a stone at point *B* is not determined by the sling to be moved, for example, along the tangent *BD*, but

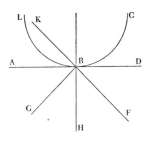

rather is moved, when the sling comes from *L* toward *B*, from the same point along a different line either inside or outside the circle, say *BF*; or along *BG* (which together with the line *BH*, drawn from the center through the circumference and cutting it at point *B*, I suppose to constitute an angle equal to the angle *FBH*) if, on the contrary, the sling is imagined to come from *C* toward *B*. Now if the stone at point *B* is supposed to be determined by the sling, which is moved in a circular direction from *L* toward *B*, to go on to be moved toward *F*, necessarily (by Axiom 18, Part II), when the sling is moved with a contrary determination from *C* toward *B*, the stone will be determined with an opposite determination to proceed to be moved along the same line *BF*, and thus tend toward *K* rather than toward *G*, which is contrary to our hypothesis. Then since no line which can be drawn through point *B* except a tangent can be constructed to make with line *BH* equal angles at the same place,[2] such as angles *DBH* and *ABH*, nothing but the tangent exists which can preserve our hypothesis, whether the sling is moved from *L* toward *B* or from *C* toward *B*; and thus no line but a tangent is to be chosen along which the stone tends to be moved.—Q.E.D.

Another Demonstration. Conceive in place of a circle the hexagon *ABH*, inscribed in a circle and having a body *C* at rest on side *AB*; then conceive a ruler *DBE* (with one end fixed

2 This is evident from *Elements*, Book III, Propositions XVIII and XIX.

at center *D,* the other end mobile) to be moved around the center *D,* cutting the line *AB* continuously. It is obvious that if the ruler *DBE,* while it is thought to be moved in this manner, meets the body *C* while cutting line *AB* at right angles,

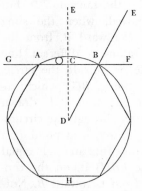

the ruler through its own impulse will determine the body *C* to proceed to be moved along the line *FBAG* toward *G,* that is, along the side *AB* extended indefinitely. But since we have assumed this hexagon at random, the same conclusion will have to be made of any figure which we think can be inscribed in this circle; because when the body *C,* at rest on one side of the figure, is impelled by the ruler *DBE* at the time when the ruler cuts that side at right angles, the body *C* will be determined by the ruler to proceed to be moved along that side extended indefinitely. Let us suppose then in place of a hexagon a rectilinear figure with an infinite number of sides (that is, according to the definition of Archimedes, a circle). It is obvious that the ruler *DBE,* wherever it meets body *C,* will always meet it while cutting some side of the figure at right angles; consequently, it will never meet body *C* without at the same time determining it to proceed to be moved along that side extended indefinitely. And since any side extended in any direction must always fall outside the figure, this side indefinitely extended will be tangent to a figure of infinite sides, that is, to a circle. If then we suppose in place of the ruler a sling moved in a circular direction, the sling will continually determine the stone to proceed to be moved along a tangent.—Q.E.D.

Notice that both of these demonstrations can be accommodated to any curvilinear figure.

PROPOSITION XVII

Every body which is moved in a circular direction endeavors to recede from the center of the circle it describes.

Demonstration. So long as a particular body is moved in a circular direction, it is compelled by some external cause, and when this cause ceases to act, it at once proceeds to be moved along a tangent (by the preceding proposition), all of whose points except that which touches the circle fall outside the

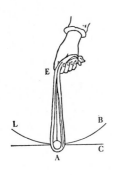

circle (by Proposition XVI, Book III, of the *Elements*), and are thus at a greater distance from the center. Therefore, when a stone, moved in a circular direction in the sling *EA*, is at point *A*, it endeavors to go on along a line whose points are all at a greater distance from the center *E* than all the points of the circumference *LAB*. But this is nothing else than to endeavor to recede from the center of the circle which it describes.—Q.E.D.

PROPOSITION XVIII

If a body *A* is moved toward another body *B* which is at rest, and *B* does not lose any of its rest through the impetus of body *A*, *A* in turn will lose none of its motion but will retain entirely the same quantity of motion it possessed at first.

Demonstration. If you deny the proposition, suppose that a body *A* loses some of its own motion without transferring what is lost into another body, say *B*. When this happens there will exist in nature a smaller quantity of motion than before, which is absurd (by Proposition XIII, Part II). The demonstration regarding rest in body *B* proceeds in the same way. This is why, if neither body transfers anything into the other body, B will retain all of its rest and A will retain all of its motion.—Q.E.D.

PROPOSITION XIX

Motion, considered in itself, differs from its determination in a particular direction, and there is no need for a moved body to rest for a time in order to be carried or repelled in an opposite direction.

Demonstration. Suppose, as in the preceding proposition, that a body A is moved directly toward B and is prevented by B from continuing further. Then (by the preceding proposition) A will retain all of its motion and will not be at rest for even the briefest instant; but although it continues to be moved, it is not moved in the same direction toward which it was first moved, since it is supposed to be impeded by B. Therefore, since its own motion remains entire while its former determination is lost, it will be moved in an opposite direction (by the remarks in Chapter II of the *Dioptrics*); consequently (by Axiom 2, Part II), determination of direction does not pertain to the essence of motion, but differs from it, and a moved body when it is repelled does not rest at all.—Q.E.D.

COROLLARY

Hence it follows that motion is not opposed to motion.

PROPOSITION XX

If a body A meets a body B and carries it along with itself, A will lose as much of its own motion as B acquires from A through their meeting.

Demonstration. If you deny the proposition, suppose that B acquires from A either more or less motion than A loses. The entire difference will have to be added or subtracted from the quantity of motion in the whole of nature, which is absurd (by Proposition XIII, Part II). Since, therefore, body B can acquire neither more nor less motion, it will acquire exactly as much as A loses.—Q.E.D.

PROPOSITION XXI

If body A is twice as large as B and is moved at an equal speed, A will have twice as much motion as B, that is, the force for maintaining a speed equal to that of B. (See figure in Proposition XX.)

Demonstration. Suppose, for example, in the place of A two B's: that is (by hypothesis), one A divided into two equal parts. Each B has the force to remain in the state in which it exists (by Proposition XIV, Part II), and the force in each (by hypothesis) is equal. If now these two B's are joined together while each retains its own rate of speed, one A will result, and its force and quantity will be equal to two B's or twice one B.—Q.E.D.

Notice that this also follows simply from the definition of motion, because the greater a moved body is, the more matter there is separated from other matter, and consequently more separation exists: that is (by Definition 8, Part II), more motion. See our fourth note regarding the definition of motion [p. 54].

PROPOSITION XXII

If a body A is equal to body B and A is moved twice as quickly as B, the force or motion in A will be twice that of B. (See figure in Proposition XX.)

Demonstration. Suppose that B acquired four degrees of speed when it first acquired the power of moving itself. If now nothing approaches, it will continue to be moved (by Proposition XIV, Part II) and to persevere in its own state. Suppose then that it acquires a new force exactly equal to its first impulse; through this it will acquire in addition to its four original degrees of speed four more degrees, which (by the same proposition) it will also preserve. That is, it will be moved twice as fast; or just as fast as A. At the same time it will possess twice as much force, or a force equal to that of A. Consequently, the motion in A is twice that in B.—Q.E.D.

Notice that by the force in moved bodies we mean the quantity of motion. This quantity in bodies of equal size ought to be greater in proportion to the speed of their motion, insofar as through that speed bodies of equal size are at a given instant farther separated from bodies immediately contiguous to them than if they were moved more slowly. Consequently (by Definition 8, Part II), they also possess more motion. In bodies at rest, however, by the force of resistance we mean the quantity of rest. From all this follows:

COROLLARY 1

The more slowly bodies are moved, the more they participate in rest, since they offer more resistance to bodies that are moved more quickly, which they meet and which possess less force than themselves; also [being less expanded], they are less separated from bodies immediately contiguous to them.

COROLLARY 2

If a body A is moved twice as quickly as a body B and B is twice as large as A, there is as much motion in the larger body B as there is in the smaller body A, and consequently an equal force as well.

Demonstration. Let B be twice as large as A while A is moved twice as quickly as B, and in addition let C be twice as small as B while being moved twice as slowly as A. Then B (by Proposition XXI, Part II) will possess twice as much motion as C, and A (by Proposition XXII, Part II) will also possess twice as much motion as *C*. Therefore (by Axiom 15, Part II), *B* and *A* have the same amount of motion, since the motion of each is double the motion of the same third body, *C*.–Q.E.D.

From the above it follows that *motion is distinct from speed.* For among bodies having the same speed, we conceive that one can possess more motion than another (by Proposition XXI, Part II); and, on the contrary, bodies of unequal speeds can possess the same amount of motion (by the preceding corollary). The same conclusion can also be drawn simply from the definition of motion, since motion is nothing other than the transfer of one body from the vicinity, and so forth.

But notice here that the third of these corollaries is not incompatible with the first. For we conceive speed in two ways: either so far as a particular body is at the same time more or less separated from the bodies immediately contiguous to it, so that it participates more or less in motion or in rest, or, to the extent that it describes in the same time a greater or smaller line, and to this extent is distinct from motion.

I could add other propositions here in fuller explanation of Proposition XIV of this part, and could explain the power of things in any condition whatsoever, as we have just done with respect to motion; but it will suffice to study Principle 43, Part Two, of the *Principles*, and to annex only one proposition which is necessary for understanding what is to follow.

PROPOSITION XXIII

When the modes of a body are forced to undergo a change, that change will always be as small as possible.

Demonstration. This proposition follows clearly enough from Proposition XIV of this part.

PROPOSITION XXIV

RULE 1

(See figure in Proposition XX.) If two bodies, say A and B, are entirely equal and are moved directly toward one another with an equal speed, then when they meet, each one will be deflected in an opposite direction without losing any speed.

It is clearly evident in this hypothesis that in order to remove the opposition of these two bodies, either both must be deflected in opposite directions or one must carry the other along with it; for they are opposed with respect to determination of direction only, and not with respect to motion.

Demonstration. When A and B meet, they must undergo some variation (by Axiom 19, Part II); but since motion is not opposed to motion (by the Corollary of Proposition XIX, Part II), they are not compelled to lose any of their motion (by Axiom 19, Part II). For this reason, the change will occur solely in their direction; but we cannot conceive that the direction of one body only, say of B, will be changed without supposing that A, by which it would have to be changed, is stronger (by Axiom 20, Part II). This, however, would be contrary to our hypothesis; thus, since the change in direction cannot occur in one body only, it will occur in both, with A and B being deflected in opposite directions (by the remarks made in Chapter II of the *Dioptrics*) while each retains all of its own motion.

PROPOSITION XXV

RULE 2

If the bodies are unequal in volume, B being larger than A (see figure in Proposition XXVII), while everything else is arranged as before, then only A will be deflected and each will continue to be moved with the same speed.

Demonstration. Since we have supposed A to be smaller than B, it will possess (by Proposition XXI, Part II) less force than B; but since in this as in the preceding hypothesis the opposition exists only in direction, the variation, as we demonstrated in the preceding proposition, must occur only in direction, and accordingly will occur only in A and not in B (by Axiom 20, Part II). Consequently, only A will be deflected in an opposite direction, by the stronger body B, and it will keep its speed unchanged.—Q.E.D.

PROPOSITION XXVI

If the bodies are unequal in volume and speed, B being twice as large as A (see figure in Proposition XXVII), while the motion in A is twice as fast as in B, with everything else arranged as before, then both will be deflected in opposite directions and each one will retain the same speed it had.

Demonstration. When A and B are moved toward one another according to the hypothesis, the same amount of motion exists in the one as in the other (by Corollary 2 of Proposition XXII, Part II); consequently, the motion of one is not opposed to the motion of the other (by the Corollary of Proposition XIX, Part II), and the forces in each are equal (by Corollary 2 of Proposition XXII, Part II). Accordingly, this hypothesis is entirely similar to the hypothesis of Proposition XXIV, Part II, and thus A and B, through the same demonstration, will be deflected in opposite directions, with each retaining all of its motion.—Q.E.D.

COROLLARY

From the three preceding propositions, it is clearly apparent that the direction of a body requires as much force, if it is to be changed, as motion; whence it follows that a body which loses more than half of its determination of direction and more than half of its motion suffers a greater change than a body which loses all of its determination.

PROPOSITION XXVII

RULE 3

If the bodies are equal in volume while B is moved somewhat

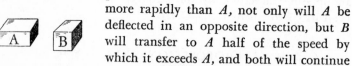

more rapidly than A, not only will A be deflected in an opposite direction, but B will transfer to A half of the speed by which it exceeds A, and both will continue to be moved with equal speed in the same direction.

Demonstration. A (by hypothesis) is opposed to B not only through its direction but also through its slowness, insofar as its slowness participates in rest (by Corollary 1 of Proposition XXII, Part II). Thus, even if it is deflected in an opposite direction and is changed only in its direction, not all of the opposition of these bodies is on that account taken away, so that (by Axiom 19, Part II) a variation should occur both in direction and in motion. But since B according to the hypothesis is moved more quickly than A, B will be (by Proposition XXII, Part II) stronger than A; consequently (by Axiom 20, Part II), a change will be produced in A by B, by which A will be deflected in an opposite direction. This was the first point.

Then so long as A is moved more slowly than B, it (by Corollary 1 of Proposition XXII, Part II) is opposed to B; therefore, a variation should take place (by Axiom 19, Part II) until A is not moved more slowly than B. However, there is nothing in the hypothesis by which A is compelled to be moved more rapidly than B, but since it cannot be moved more slowly than B, for it is impelled by B, nor more quickly than B, it therefore goes on to be moved with the same speed as B. Besides, if B should transfer less than half of its excess speed to A, then A would continue to be moved more slowly than B. But if B transfers more than half of its excess speed to A, then A will proceed to be moved more rapidly than B. But both conditions are absurd, as we have just demonstrated. Therefore, a variation occurs in both of them, until B has transferred to A the half of its excess speed which (by Proposition XX, Part II) it ought to lose; and so both will proceed to be moved without any opposition at the same speed in the same direction.—Q.E.D.

COROLLARY

It follows from this that the more quickly a body is moved, the more it is determined to continue to be moved along the line on which it is being moved; and, on the contrary, the more slowly it is moved, the less its direction is determined.

SCHOLIUM

Lest the reader confuse the force of determination with the force of motion, it seemed well to add here a few remarks explicitly distinguishing the force of determination from the force of motion. Accordingly, if the bodies A and C are regarded as equal and as being moved directly toward one another at equal speeds, both of them (by Proposition XXIV, Part II) will be deflected in opposite directions while retaining all of their own motions. But

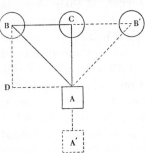

if body C is at point B and is moved obliquely toward A, it is perfectly clear that it is then less determined to be moved along line BD or CA than along BA. Thus, although C has a motion equal to that of A, still the force of determination in C when it is moved directly toward A—a force equal to the force of determination in A—is greater than the force of determination in C when C is moved from B toward A, and it is as much greater as the line BA is longer than line CA. For the more the line BA exceeds in length the line CA, the more time is required for a body at B (the bodies at B and A being supposed here to be moved at equal speeds) to be moved along line BD or CA, through which it is opposed to the direction of the body at A. Accordingly, when C meets A obliquely from B, it will be determined just as it would should it continue to be moved along line AB' toward B' (which I suppose, when it is at the point at which line AB' cuts the prolongation of line BC, to be as far from C as C is from B). But A, while retaining the whole of its motion and determination, will continue to be moved toward C and will drive body B along with itself, since B, so long as it is determined to be moved along the diagonal AB' and is moved with a speed equal to that of A, requires more time than A to describe through its own motion any part of the line AC. To this extent it is opposed to the determination of body A, which is the stronger body. But that the force of determination in C moved from B toward A, insofar as it participates in the line CA, may be equal to the force of determination of C moved directly toward A (a force equal by hypothesis to that of A), B will necessarily have to possess as many more degrees of motion than A as the line BA has more parts than the line CA. Then when B meets the body A obliquely, A will be deflected toward A', and B in an opposite direction, toward B', while both will retain the whole of their own motions. But if the excess of B's motion over A's is greater than the excess of line BA over line CA, then B will repel A toward A', and it will contribute some of its own motion to A until its motion is in the same proportion to A's motion as the line BA is to the line CA, and it will go on to be moved in the direction in which it first moved, less the amount of motion it transferred to A. For example, if line AC is to line AB as 1 is to 2, and if the motion of body A is to the motion of body B as 1 is to 5, then B will transfer into A one degree of its own motion and will repel it in an opposite direction, and B will continue to be moved in the same direction in which it originally tended with its four remaining degrees of motion.

PROPOSITION XXVIII

Rule 4

If a body A (see figure in Proposition XXVII) is entirely at rest and is somewhat larger than B, then with whatever speed B is moved toward A, B will never move A but will be repelled by A in an opposite direction while retaining the whole of its motion.

Notice that the opposition of these bodies is removed in three ways: when one body carries the other along with it so that afterwards they proceed to be moved at the same speed in the same direction; or, when one body is deflected in an opposite direction, while the other retains the whole of its rest; or, when the one is deflected in an opposite direction, and transfers some of its motion into the body at rest. A fourth condition does not exist (by virtue of Proposition XIII, Part II). Thus it will have to be demonstrated (by Proposition XXIII, Part II) that according to our hypothesis the least possible change takes place in these bodies.

Demonstration. If B were to move A until both would proceed to be moved at the same speed, B (by Proposition XX, Part II) would have to transfer into A as much of its own motion as A acquires, and (by Proposition XXI, Part II) would have to lose more than half of its own motion, and consequently (by the Corollary of Proposition XXVII, Part II), more than half of its determination as well. Thus (by the Corollary of Proposition XXVI, Part II), it would undergo a greater change than if it lost only its determination. And if A should lose some of its rest but not enough for it to go on to be moved with the same speed as B, then the opposition of these two bodies will not be removed; for A through its slowness, insofar as slowness participates in rest (by Corollary 1 of Proposition XXII, Part II), will be in opposition to B's speed, and so B in this state will have to be deflected in an opposite direction, losing all of its determination and that part of its

motion which it transferred into A. This, of course, is a
greater change than the loss of its determination alone. The
change then, as required by our hypothesis, is the least that
can exist in these bodies, because it is a change in determination only; accordingly (by Proposition XXIII, Part II), no
other takes place.—Q.E.D.

Notice in the demonstration of this proposition that the
same thing occurs in other cases: for example, we have not
cited Proposition XIX of Part Two, in which it is demonstrated that the direction can be entirely changed, while the
motion, nevertheless, remains the same. This should, however,
be kept in mind if the force of the present demonstration is to
be correctly perceived. For in Proposition XXIII of Part Two,
we did not say that the variation will always be an absolute
minimum, but the least that can exist. From Proposition
XVIII, Part Two and Proposition XIX, Part Two with its
corollary, it is obvious that a change consisting solely in determination can exist.

PROPOSITION XXIX

RULE 5

If a body A (see figure in Proposition XXX) at rest is smaller
than B, then however slowly B is moved toward A, it will carry
A along with itself, while transferring to A as much of its motion as is needed for both to be moved afterwards at the same
speed. (Read *Principles,* Part II, Principle 50.)

In this rule as in the preceding one, only three conditions
can be conceived in which this opposition would be removed.
But we will demonstrate that the change supposed by our
hypothesis is the least possible change to take place in these
bodies, and accordingly (by Proposition XXIII, Part II) that
they must change in this manner.

Demonstration. According to our hypothesis, B transfers into
A (by Proposition XXI, Part II) less than half of its own motion and (by the Corollary of Proposition XXVII, Part II)

less than half of its determination. But if *B* did not carry *A* along with itself, and instead was deflected in a contrary direction, it would lose all of its determination and a greater variation would take place (by the Corollary of Proposition XXVI, Part II); and a still greater variation would occur if *B* lost all of its determination together with part of its motion, as is supposed in the third condition. Consequently, the variation according to our hypothesis is the least possible.—Q.E.D.

PROPOSITION XXX

RULE 6

If a body *A* at rest is as equal as possible to a body *B* moved toward it, it will in part be impelled by *B* and will in part repel *B* in an opposite direction.

Here too, as in the preceding, only three cases can be conceived; accordingly it will have to be demonstrated that we posit here the least variation that can exist.

Demonstration. If body *B* should carry body *A* along with itself until both proceed to be moved at equal speeds, then there would be as much motion in the one as in the other (by Proposition XXII, Part II), and (by the Corollary of Proposition XXVII, Part II) *B* will have to lose half of its determination and (by Proposition XX, Part II) half of its motion as well. But if it is repelled by *A* in an opposite direction, then it will lose all of its determination and will retain the whole of its motion (by Proposition XVIII, Part II). This variation is equal to the former one (by the Corollary of Proposition XXVI, Part II). But neither of these can occur, for if *A* should retain its own status and could change the determination of *B*, it would necessarily (by Axiom 20, Part II) be stronger than *B*, which would be contrary to our hypothesis. And if *B* should carry *A* along with itself until both were moved at equal speeds, *B* would be stronger than *A*, and this also is against our hypothesis. Since, therefore, neither of these cases can take place, the third occurs, namely, that B will to some extent impel A and will to some extent be repelled by A.—Q.E.D. (Read *Principles,* Part II, Principle 51.)

PROPOSITION XXXI

Rule 7

If B and A are moved in the same direction, A moving slowly and B following it more rapidly so as finally to catch it, and if A is larger than B while the excess of speed in B is larger than the excess of size in A, then B will transfer enough of its motion into A for both to proceed afterwards at the same speed in the same direction. But if, on the contrary, the excess of size in A is larger than the excess of speed in B, then B will be deflected in an opposite direction by A, although retaining all of its motion.

Read *Principles,* Part Two, Principle 52. Here again, as before, only three cases can be conceived.

Demonstration of the First Part. Since (by Propositions XXI and XXII, Part II) B is supposed to be the stronger, it cannot be deflected in an opposite direction by A (by Axiom 20, Part II); therefore, since B is the stronger, it will move A along with itself and, indeed, in such a way that both will proceed to be moved at equal speeds. For in this way the least change will take place, as is easily apparent from the remarks above.

Demonstration of the Second Part. B cannot (by Axiom 20, Part II) impel A, which (by Propositions XXI and XXII, Part II) is supposed to be stronger than it is, and it cannot give to A any of its motion; consequently (by the Corollary of Proposition XIV, Part II), B will retain all of its motion but will not move in the same direction because it is supposed to be impeded by A. Therefore (by the remarks in Chapter II of the *Dioptrics*), it will be deflected in an opposite direction, while preserving all of its motion (by Proposition XVIII, Part II).—Q.E.D.

Notice that here and in the preceding propositions we have assumed, as though it were demonstrated, that every body directly striking another body by which it is absolutely impeded from proceeding farther in the same direction must be deflected in an opposite direction, not just any direction. To understand this, read Chapter II of the *Dioptrics*.

Thus far, in explaining the changes which occur in bodies through their mutual impulse, we have considered two bodies as though they were divided from all bodies: that is, no account has been taken of the bodies surrounding them on every side. Now, however, we will consider their status and changes in relation to the bodies by which they are surrounded on every side.

PROPOSITION XXXII

If a body *B* is surrounded on every side by moved particles impelling it with an equal force at one time in all directions, *B* will remain unmoved in the same place so long as no other cause intervenes.

Demonstration. This proposition is self-evident. For if *B* were moved in a particular direction by the impulse of particles coming from one side, the particles that move it would drive it with a greater force than others impelling it at the same time in an opposite direction, so that these could not produce their proper effect (by Axiom 20, Part II). But this would be contrary to our hypothesis.

PROPOSITION XXXIII

With the particles arranged as above, body *B* could be moved in any direction by the addition of a force, however small.

Demonstration. All the bodies immediately touching *B*, since (by hypothesis) they are in motion while *B* (by the preceding proposition) remains unmoved, as soon as they touch B will be deflected in a different direction, while retaining all of their motion (by Proposition XXVIII, Part II). Accordingly, body B is continually and spontaneously abandoned by the bodies immediately contiguous to it. However large, therefore, B is imagined to be, no action is required to separate it from the bodies immediately touching it (by the fourth note to Definition 8, Part II). Consequently, no external force however small can be impressed on B which is not larger than the force which B possesses for remaining in the same place (since B has no power of adhering to the bodies immediately touching it, as we demonstrated just now), and which, being added to the impulse of the particles that drive B in a particular direction, is not greater than the force of the other particles driving B in an opposite direction (for without the addition of this new force, the two forces were supposed to be equal). Therefore (by Axiom 20, Part II), B will be moved in any direction whatsoever by this additional force, however small it is assumed to be.—Q.E.D.

PROPOSITION XXXIV

When the other bodies are arranged as above, body B cannot be moved more quickly than the additional force by which it is impelled, even though the particles by which it is surrounded are agitated far more rapidly.

Demonstration. Even if the particles, which together with an additional force drive B in a certain direction, are agitated much more rapidly than the additional force, still, since (by hypothesis) they possess no greater force than the bodies which repel B in an opposite direction, they expend all the force of their own determination simply in resisting those bodies and do not contribute any speed to B (by Proposition XXXII, Part II). Therefore, since no other circumstances or causes are supposed, B will receive no speed from any cause other than the external force, and accordingly (by Axiom 8, Part I) could not be moved more rapidly than it is driven by the external force. —Q.E.D.

PROPOSITION XXXV

When body *B* is moved as above by an external impulse, it takes most of its motion from the bodies by which it is continually surrounded, and not from the external force.

Demonstration. Body *B,* however large, must be moved (by Proposition XXXIII, Part II) by an impulse, however small. Let us suppose then that *B* is four times as large as the external body by whose force it is driven; since (by the preceding proposition) both should be moved at equal speeds, there will be four times as much motion in *B* as there is in the external body by which it is driven (by Proposition XXI, Part II); consequently (by Axiom 8, Part I), it does not take the principal part of its motion from the external force. Further, since apart from the external force no other causes are assumed except the bodies by which it is continually surrounded (since *B* is supposed to be immobile in itself), *B* takes (by Axiom 7, Part I) the greater part of its motion solely from these bodies and not from the external force.—Q.E.D.

Notice that we cannot say here, as above, that the motion of particles coming from one direction is needed for resisting the motion of particles coming from the opposite direction. For bodies moved (as these bodies are supposed) with an equal motion toward one another are contrary only in determination,[3] not in motion (by the Corollary of Proposition XIX, Part II); thus they expend only their determination in resisting one another, not their motion. Besides, body *B* cannot take any determination, nor consequently (by the Corollary of Proposition XXVII, Part II) any speed, so far as that is distinct from motion, from the bodies lying about it. But it does

[3] See Prop. XXIV, Part II. There it is demonstrated that two bodies resisting one another expend their determination, but not their motion.

receive motion; and indeed, when an additional force is added, it must necessarily be moved by these surrounding bodies, as we have demonstrated in this proposition and as is easy to see from the way in which we demonstrated Proposition XXXIII, Part Two.

PROPOSITION XXXVI

If a particular body, our hand for example, can be moved with an equal motion in every direction, so that it does not resist other bodies in any way and so that other bodies do not resist it in any way, then in the space through which the hand would be so moved, as many bodies will necessarily be moved in one direction as in any other, with a force of speed equal among the various bodies and equal to that of the hand.

Demonstration. No body can be moved through any space which is not filled with bodies (by Proposition III, Part II). Accordingly, I claim that the space through which our hand can be moved in this way is filled with bodies which will be moved within the conditions I have described. If you deny this, assume that the bodies either are at rest or are moved in some other fashion. If they are at rest, they will necessarily resist the motion of the hand (by Proposition XIV, Part II), until its motion is communicated to them so that finally they are moved in the same direction and at the same speed as the hand (by Proposition XX, Part II). But in our hypothesis they are supposed not to resist; therefore, these bodies are moved. This was the first point.

Next, they ought to be moved in all directions. If you deny this, assume that there is some particular direction, say from *A* toward *B,* in which they are not moved. If then the hand is moved from *A* toward *B,* it will necessarily meet the bodies that are moved (by the first part of this demonstration), and moved, according to your hypothesis, with a determination different from that of the hand. Consequently, they will resist it (by Proposition XIV, Part II) until they are moved in the same direction as the hand (by Proposition XXIV and the Scholium to Proposition XXVII, Part II). But (according to our hypothesis) they do not resist the hand, and therefore they will be moved in any direction whatever. This was the second point.

Again, these bodies will be moved in any direction whatever with an equal force of speed. Supposing that they are not moved with an equal force of speed, assume that those which are moved from A toward B are moved with a force of speed less than that of those which are moved from A toward

C. In these circumstances, if the hand were moved from A toward B with the same speed with which the bodies are moved from A toward C (since it is supposed that the hand can be moved with an equal motion in all directions without resistance), the bodies moved from A toward B will resist the hand (by Proposition XIV, Part II) until they are moved with a force of speed equal to that of the hand (by Proposition XXXI, Part II). But this is contrary to the hypothesis; therefore, they will be moved with an equal force of speed in all directions. This was the third point.

Finally, if the bodies are moved with a force of speed not equal to that of the hand, then the hand will be moved either more slowly and with less force of speed, or more quickly and with a greater force of speed, than the other bodies. If more slowly, the hand will resist the bodies following it in the same direction (by Proposition XXXI, Part II). If more quickly, the bodies which the hand follows and with which it is moved in the same direction will resist it (by the same proposition). Both cases are against the hypothesis. Therefore, since the hand can be moved neither more slowly nor more quickly, it will be moved with the same force of speed as the bodies.— Q.E.D.

If you wonder why I say "the same force of speed" and not simply "the same speed," read the Scholium to the Corollary of Proposition XXVII, Part Two. If then you ask whether the

hand while it is moved, for example, from *A* toward *B* does
not resist the bodies moved with an equal force at the same
time from *B* toward *A*, read Proposition XXXIII, Part Two,
from which you will understand that their force balances the
force of the bodies which are moved from *A* toward *B* at the
same time as the hand (for through the third part of this
proposition these two forces are equal).

PROPOSITION XXXVII

If a particular body, say *A*, can be moved in any direction by
a force however small, it is necessarily surrounded by bodies
all moved with an equal speed.

Demonstration. Body *A* must be bound on every side by bodies
(by Proposition VI, Part II), and these bodies must be moved
equally in all directions. For if they
were at rest, body *A* could not be
moved in any direction (as is supposed) by a force however
small, but only by such a force as could move with itself the
bodies immediately touching *A* (by Axiom 20, Part II). Then,
if the bodies by which *A* is surrounded were moved by a
greater force in one direction rather than another, say from *B*
toward *C* rather than from *C* toward *B*, since *A* is bound on
every side by moved bodies (as we have just demonstrated),
necessarily (through the demonstration of Proposition XXXIII,
Part II) the bodies moved from *B* toward *C* will carry *A* along
with themselves in that direction. Accordingly, not any small
force will suffice to move *A* toward *B*, but only a force which
could make up the excess motion in the bodies coming from *B*
toward *C* (by Axiom 20, Part II); consequently, the bodies
surrounding *A* must be moved with an equal force in all directions.—Q.E.D.

SCHOLIUM

Since these remarks relate to bodies which are called "fluids,"
it follows that fluid bodies are those which are divided into

many tiny particles moved with an equal force in all directions. Although these particles cannot be seen by the keenest eye, still what we have now clearly demonstrated should not have to be denied. For such subtlety of nature as cannot be determined or attained by any thought (to say nothing of the senses) is sufficiently overcome by the remarks in Propositions X and XI, Part Two. Moreover, since it is sufficiently established above that bodies resist other bodies solely through their rest, and that in hardness, as the senses indicate, we perceive nothing other than that the parts of hard bodies resist the motion of our hands, we clearly conclude that those bodies, all of whose parts immediately adjoining one another are at rest, are hard. (Read Principles 54 through 56 of Part II of the *Principles*.)

PART THREE

Now that we have expounded the most universal principles of natural things, we must go on to explain the things which follow from them. Yet since more things follow from these principles than our minds can ever embrace in thought and since we are not determined by them to consider one thing rather than another, a brief account must first be presented of the principal phenomena whose causes we shall investigate in this section. This account is found in Principles 5 to 15 of Part Three of the *Principles*. Also, from Principles 20 to 43 the hypothesis is proposed which Descartes thought most suitable not only for understanding the phenomena of the heavens but also for investigating their natural causes.

Furthermore, since the best way to understand the nature of plants or of men is to consider how they were gradually born and begotten from seeds, it will be necessary to discover through thought principles which are entirely simple and easy to understand. We shall then be able to demonstrate that the stars, and the earth, and all the things which we survey in the visible universe could have arisen from these principles as though from a few seeds, even though we know that they were never produced in this way. In so doing we will explain their nature far better than by simply describing the sort of things that they now are.

I say that we are looking for simple principles, easy to understand, for unless they are that, they will obviously be of no use to us, since we are imagining these seminal causes of things only to understand the nature of things more easily and to move, as mathematicians do, from the very clear to the more obscure, and from the very simple to the more complex.

We claim, then, to be looking for principles by means of which to demonstrate how the stars and earth, and all the rest, could have arisen. For we do not, as astronomers often do, seek causes which suffice to explain only the phenomena of the heavens; rather, we seek causes which lead us to a knowledge of things on earth as well (because in our opinion everything that we observe taking place on the surface of the earth must be reckoned among the phenomena of nature). In order to find such principles, the following conditions must be observed in a good hypothesis:

1. That (considered simply in itself) it contain no contradiction.

2. That it be as simple as possible.

3. That, as a consequence of the second condition, it be easy to understand.

4. That everything observed in the whole of nature be deducible from it.

We said, finally, that in order to deduce the phenomena of nature as from a cause, it is permissible to assume a hypothesis, even if we know that the phenomena were never actually produced according to it. That this may be understood I will use the following example. If someone should find traced on a paper a curved line, say a parabola, and should want to investigate its nature, it would be entirely indifferent whether he supposed that line to have been cut previously from a cone and then imprinted on the paper, or described by the motion of two straight lines, or produced in some other manner, so long as he demonstrated from his supposition all the properties of the parabola. In fact, even if he knew that the line had been made on the paper from the imprint of a conic section, he could nevertheless at his pleasure fashion a different cause, if this seemed to him more convenient for explaining all the properties of the parabola. In the same way, we can assume at our pleasure a hypothesis for explaining the outlines of nature, so long as we deduce from it in a mathematical sequence all the phenomena of nature. What is even more remarkable, we could scarcely assume anything from which we could not deduce, through the help of the laws of nature explained above, effects which are entirely the same, although we could possibly make our task more laborious. For, since with the help of these laws matter assumes successively all the forms of which it is capable, if we consider these forms in order we can at length arrive at the form which is the present form of the universe. Thus, we need have no fear of error through the assumption of a false hypothesis.

POSTULATE

Let it be granted that all the matter of which this visible universe is composed was in the beginning divided by God into approximately equal particles; not, however, into spherical particles, since several round bodies joined together do not fill a continuous space, but into parts differently figured, moderate in size, striking a mean between the particles of which the heavens and stars are now composed. Suppose then that these particles possessed as much motion in themselves as is now found in the universe, and were moved with an equal force, each about its own center and independently of the rest, so that together they composed a fluid body of the sort we think the heavens are now. Then suppose also that a great number of particles were moved about certain other points, equally distant from one another and arranged in the same manner as the centers of the fixed stars are now, while others were moved about still other points, equal in number to the planets. In this way they would have composed as many different vortices as there are stars now in the universe. (See the figure in Principle 47, Part III, of the *Principles*.)

This hypothesis considered in itself implies no contradiction, since it attributes nothing to matter but divisibility and motion, modifications which, as we have already demonstrated, really exist in matter. Also, since we have shown that matter is indefinite and entirely the same in both heaven and earth, we can suppose without risk of contradiction that these modifications have existed in the whole of matter.

The hypothesis is, moreover, perfectly simple, because it supposes no inequality or dissimilarity in the particles into which matter was first divided, nor does it suppose any difference in their motion. Thus the hypothesis is also very easy to understand. The same conclusions are obvious from the fact that the hypothesis supposes nothing to have existed in matter which is not immediately known to anyone simply from the concept of matter, namely, its divisibility and local motion.

Nevertheless, we shall attempt to show that everything observed in nature can actually be deduced, as far as possible, from this hypothesis, and we shall make the attempt in the following order. First, we shall deduce the fluidity of the heavens and show how this is the cause of light. Next, we shall consider the nature of the sun and, at the same time, the things observed in the fixed stars. Afterwards, we shall discuss comets, and finally the planets with their phenomena.

DEFINITIONS

1. By an *ecliptic* we mean that part of a vortex which describes the greatest circle as it gyrates about its axis.

2. By *poles* we mean the parts of a vortex which are farthest removed from the ecliptic, or the parts which describe the smallest circle.

3. By the *endeavor to move* [*conatus ad motum*], we do not mean a particular intention; rather, we mean that a part of matter is so situated and prone to move that it would actually move in some direction if it were not prevented by a cause.

4. By an *angle* we mean anything in a body which projects beyond a spherical figure.

AXIOMS

1. Several round bodies joined together cannot occupy a continuous space.

2. A portion of matter divided into angular parts, if the parts are moved about their own centers, requires a larger space than it would if all the parts were at rest and all their sides directly touched one another.

3. The smaller a part of matter is, the more easily it is divided by a given force.

4. Parts of matter which are in motion in the same direction, and which do not recede from one another in that motion, are not actually divided.

PROPOSITION I

The parts into which matter was first divided were angular, not round.

Demonstration. The whole of matter was from the beginning divided into equal and similar parts (by the Postulate of Part III); therefore (by Axiom 1, Part III, and Proposition II, Part II), they were not round; and so (by Definition 4, Part III), angular.—Q.E.D.

PROPOSITION II

The force which caused particles of matter to be moved about their own centers caused at the same time the angles of the particles to wear away by their mutual contact.

Demonstration. The whole of matter was in the beginning divided into equal (by the Postulate of Part III) and angular (by Proposition I, Part III) parts. If, therefore, as soon as they began to be moved about their own centers their angles had not been worn down, necessarily (by Axiom 2, Part III) the whole of matter must have occupied a greater space than when it was at rest. But this is absurd (by Proposition IV, Part II); therefore, their angles were worn down as soon as they began to be moved.—Q.E.D.

(The rest is lacking.) [1]

---

[1] [See Louis Meyer's Preface, pp. 6-7.]

AN APPENDIX

containing

THOUGHTS ON METAPHYSICS

in which the more difficult questions which occur in Metaphysics, both in its General and Special parts, concerning
Being and its Affections, God and his Attributes, and
human Mind, are briefly explained.

PART ONE

In which the principal topics which commonly occur in general Metaphysics, concerning Being and its Affections, are briefly explained.[1]

CHAPTER I

CONCERNING REAL BEING, FICTION, AND LOGICAL BEING

I say nothing of the definition of this science or of the object that it studies; my only purpose here is to explain those things which, although somewhat obscure, are treated in various places by authors of metaphysical works.

1. *Definition of Being.* Let us begin therefore with being, by which I mean *everything which, when it is clearly and distinctly perceived, we find exists necessarily or at least can exist.*

2. *Chimeras, fictions, and logical beings are not real beings.* But from the above definition or, if you prefer, description, it follows that chimeras [*Chimaera*], fiction [*Ens fictum*], and logical beings [*Ens rationis*] cannot be classified as beings. For a chimera [2] by its own nature cannot exist. Fiction [*Ens fictum*], in turn, excludes clear and distinct perception, because in forming fictions a man simply through the exercise of his

1 [In the Dutch translation of 1664, there is the following addition:
The end and object of this part is to demonstrate that logic and the philosophy in common use serve only to exercise and strengthen memory, so that it can retain well things that are met without order or connection between them, things which are perceived through the senses and by which we cannot be affected save through the senses; but these disciplines do not serve to exercise the understanding.

For this translation of the Dutch I am indebted to the French translation of Roland Caillois, in *Spinoza Œuvres Complètes,* tr. R. Caillois, M. Francès, and R. Misrahi (Paris, 1954), p. 300.]

2 Notice here and in what follows that by "chimera" is meant that whose nature involves an obvious contradiction, as is more fully explained in Chapter III.

freedom—and not, as in error, unknowingly—prudently and knowingly joins what he wants to join and disjoins what he wants to disjoin. Lastly, logical being [*Ens Rationis*] is nothing but a mode of thinking which helps us retain, explain, and imagine more easily things already understood. Notice that by the phrase "mode of thinking" we mean, as we have already explained in the Scholium to Proposition IV, Part One, all the affections of thought, such as understanding, joy, imagination, and so forth.

3. *By what modes of thought we retain things.* That there exist, however, certain modes of thinking which help us to remember things more firmly and easily, and to recall them when we wish, and to consider them steadily, is evident to those who use that familiar rule of memory by which we are advised, in order to retain a new object and impress it upon the memory, to refer it to something else with which we are already familiar and which in name or in fact agrees with the new object. In this way philosophers reduce all natural objects to determinate classes to which they refer anything new that occurs to them, and these classes they call *genus, species,* and so forth.

4. *By what modes of thought we explain things.* For explaining a thing we also have modes of thought, which consist in determining a thing by comparing it with something else. The modes of thought through which we accomplish this are called *time, number,* and *measure,* and whatever others there are of this sort. Of these, time serves for explaining duration, number for discrete quantity, and measure for continuous quantity.

5. *By what modes of thought we imagine things.* Finally, since we are in the habit of depicting to ourselves by some sort of image in our imagination the things we understand, it comes about that we imagine positively things which do not exist in the likeness of things actually existing. For the mind, considered solely in itself as a thinking thing, has no greater power for affirming than for denying; but since imagining is simply sensing the traces to be found in the brain from the

motion of vital spirits—this motion being excited in the senses by external objects—such a sensation can be nothing but a confused affirmation. Hence it follows that we imagine as real things all the modes which the mind uses for negations, such as blindness, extremity, end, boundary, darkness, and so forth.

6. *Why logical entities are not ideas of things, yet are taken for them.* From the above it is clear that these modes of thinking are not ideas of things and cannot be classified as ideas; for this reason also they have no object [*ideatum*] which necessarily exists or can exist. But these modes of thinking are taken for ideas of things because they originate and spring so directly from ideas of real things that they can very easily be confused, one with the other, by those who do not observe them very carefully. This is why people have given them names as though these modes signified beings existing outside our mind, and these beings, or rather nonbeings, they call "logical beings."

7. *Being is improperly divided into real and logical.* From this it is easy to see how inept is the division of being into real and logical: it divides being into being and not-being, or into being and mode of thinking. Yet I do not marvel that verbalizing or grammatical philosophers fall into such errors; for they judge things by their names, not names by things.

8. *How logical being can be called "mere nothing" and also "real being."* He speaks no less ineptly who denies that logical being is mere nothing. For if he seeks outside his intellect what is signified by these words, he will find that it is mere nothing; if, however, he means by these words our modes of thinking, these are in truth real entities. For when I ask what *species* is, I seek nothing but the nature of this particular mode of thinking which really is a being and is distinct from other modes of thinking; but these modes of thinking cannot be called ideas nor can they be said to be true or false, any more than love can be called true or false, but only good or bad. Thus Plato, when he said that man is a two-footed animal without feathers, was no more in error than those who said that man is a rational animal. For Plato was no less aware than others that man is a rational animal, but he referred man to this particular class

to be able, whenever he wanted to think about man, at once
to enter upon a meditation by referring to a class which he was
easily able to recollect. Aristotle, on the other hand, was very
gravely in error if he supposed that he had adequately explained human essence through that definition of his.[3] Whether
Plato did well can also be asked. But this is not the place for
that.

9. *In investigating things, real beings must not be confused
with logical beings.* From all that has been said it appears that
there is no correspondence between real being and the objects
[*ideata*] of logical being. Thus it is easy to see how sedulously
we must take care not to confuse real and logical beings when
we investigate things. For it is one thing to investigate the
nature of things and quite another to inquire into the modes
through which we perceive them. If these are confused, we
shall be unable to understand either our modes of perceiving
or nature itself. Indeed, what is most important, such confusion will cause us to fall into enormous errors, as has happened to many before now.

10. *How logical being and fiction are distinguished.* It
should be noticed that many people confuse logical being with
fiction; they suppose that fiction is logical being because it has
no existence outside the mind. But if the definitions of logical
being and fiction are rightly examined, as they were just now
given, a great difference will be discovered between the two
both by reason of their cause and also from the nature of each
without regard to their cause. For we have said that a fiction
is nothing other than two terms joined solely by the will without the guidance of reason; consequently, a fiction can be true
by chance. Logical being, however, does not depend simply
upon will nor does it consist in the conjunction of terms, as is
sufficiently manifest from the definition. If, then, someone

[3] [Plato's classification of man as a featherless biped occurs in *Statesman*,
266 ff., where the classification is called a "jest." Aristotle's definition of
man as an animal that "acts in accordance with rational principle" is de-
veloped throughout the *Nicomachean Ethics,* and also in the *Politics,*
especially 1260a.]

should ask whether fiction is real being or logical being, we could do nothing but recall and repeat what we have already said: namely, that it is improper to divide being into real being and logical being. Accordingly, the question whether fiction is real or logical being is asked on poor grounds, for it supposes that all being is divided into real and logical.

11. *The division of being*. But let us return to our subject, from which we seem somehow to have digressed. From the definition or, if you prefer, description already given of being, it is easy to see that being should be divided into being which exists necessarily of its own nature, so that its essence entails existence, and into being whose essence entails only possible existence. This last is divided into substance and mode, whose definitions are given in Principles 51, 52, and 56 of Part One of the *Principles of Philosophy,* so that there is no need to repeat them here. I wish only to point out regarding this division that we expressly say: being is divided into substance and mode, but not into substance and accident. For accident is only a mode of thinking, which does no more than denote an aspect. For example, when I say that a triangle is moved, motion is not a mode of the triangle but of the body which is moved; consequently, in respect of the triangle, motion is called accident, but in respect of body it is a real being or a mode, since motion cannot be conceived without body but can indeed be conceived without triangle.

Now, that what has already been said and what is to follow may be better understood, we shall try to explain what is to be understood by the being of essence [*esse essentiae*], the being of existence [*esse existentiae*], the being of idea [*esse ideae*], and, finally, the being of power [*esse potentiae*]. We are moved to this discussion by the ignorance of those who see no distinction between essence and existence, or who, if they do recognize it, confuse the being of essence with the being of idea or the being of power. So to satisfy both them and the subject matter, we shall explain the matter as distinctly as we can in what follows.

CHAPTER II

THE BEING OF ESSENCE; OF EXISTENCE; OF IDEA; AND OF POWER

1. *Creatures exist in God eminently.* To see clearly what is to be understood by these four concepts of being, it is only necessary to place before ourselves what we have already said about uncreated substance or God:

First, God contains eminently [4] what is found in created things formally; that is, God possesses attributes in which all created attributes are contained, but in a more eminent mode (see Axiom 8 and Corollary 1 of Proposition XII, Part I). For example, we clearly form a concept of extension without existence, and since extension lacks any force in itself for existing, we demonstrated that it was created by God (Proposition XXI, Part I). Besides, since there must be at least as much perfection in a cause as in its effect, it follows that all the perfections of extension are in God. But since we afterwards saw that an extended thing is by its own nature divisible—that is, contains imperfection—for this reason we were not able to attribute extension to God (Part I, Proposition XVI), and accordingly we were driven to confess that there exists in God some particular attribute which contains all the perfections of matter in a more excellent manner (Scholium to Proposition IX, Part I), and which can take the place of matter.

Second, God understands himself and all else besides; that is, he contains everything in himself objectively [5] (Proposition IX, Part I).

Third, God is the cause of all things, and he acts with absolute freedom of will.

2. *What the beings of essence, existence, idea, and power are.* From these explanations it is clear what must be understood by

[4] [That is, God contains in himself all the reality and perfection of creatures more perfectly than they themselves do. See Part I, Axiom 8, where the words "eminently" and "formally" are discussed.]

[5] [Objectively: as an object of thought.]

these four concepts of being. First, *the being of essence* is nothing but that mode in which created things are comprehended in the attributes of God; then, *the being of idea* is used to refer to things according as they are all contained objectively in the idea of God; further, *the being of power* is mentioned only with regard to the power of God, by which he could create with absolute freedom of will all the things not yet existing; and, finally, *the being of existence* is the very essence of things considered apart from God and in themselves, and is attributed to things after their creation by God.

3. *These four beings are not distinct except in creatures.* From these considerations it appears clearly that these four beings are not to be distinguished from one another except in created things and are in no manner distinct in God. For we do not think that God has been potentially in another, and his existence and understanding are not to be distinguished from his essence.

4. *Replies to some questions about essence.* On these grounds, we can reply easily to questions which are sometimes asked about essence, questions such as the following: whether essence should be distinguished from existence; and if it should, whether it is something different from idea; and if it is, whether it has any being external to the intellect. The last question must, obviously, be answered affirmatively. To the first, however, we reply with the distinction that in God essence is not distinct from existence, since his essence cannot be conceived without existence; but in everything else essence differs from existence and most certainly can be thought of without existence. But to the second question we reply that a thing which can be clearly and distinctly, that is, truly, conceived as external to the intellect is something different from idea. But the question is then asked whether that being which is external to the intellect exists in itself or whether it was created by God. To this we reply that formal essence does not exist of itself, nor yet is it created, for these both suppose that the thing actually exists; but formal essence depends solely on the divine essence in which all things are contained; and, in

this sense, we agree with those who say that the essences of things are eternal. At this point, it can be asked how we would know the essences of things before knowing the nature of God, since essences, as we just said, depend solely on the nature of God. To this I reply that our knowing the essences of things arises because things have already been created; for if they had not been created, I would straightway concede that our knowing them would be impossible until we had attained an adequate conception of God's nature. Indeed, it would be just as impossible or even more impossible than knowing the nature of the ordinates of a parabola before the nature of the parabola had been noted.

5. *Why the author refers to the attributes of God in defining essence.* Furthermore, it should be noted that although the essences of modes not existing are comprehended in their substances and although the *being of the essence* of these modes is in their substances, still we have wanted to refer to God in order to explain the essence of modes and substances generally, and also because the essence of modes was not in the substances of these modes except after the substances were created, and we were seeking the eternal *being of essences.*

6. *Why the author did not examine the definitions of other authors.* I do not think it worthwhile here to refute the authors who think other than we do, nor even to examine their definitions or descriptions of essence and existence, for in this way we should make a clear subject obscure. For what can be clearer than to know what essence and existence are, seeing that we cannot give a definition of anything without at the same time explaining its essence.

7. *An easy way to learn the distinction between essence and existence.* And finally, if any philosopher still doubts whether essence is to be distinguished from existence in created things, there is no need to labor the definitions of essence and existence in order to remove his doubt; for if he simply approaches people who make statuary or work in wood, they will show him how they have in detail the idea of a statue not yet exist-

ing, and afterwards they will exhibit it to him in actual existence.

CHAPTER III

CONCERNING THE NECESSARY, IMPOSSIBLE, POSSIBLE, AND CONTINGENT

1. *What is meant here by affections.* Having thus explained the nature of being, so far as it is being, we pass on to the explanation of some of its affections, wherein it should be noted that we understand here by affections what Descartes on a different occasion (in Principle 52, Part I of the *Principles*) called "attributes." For being, so far as it is being, like substance does not affect us through itself alone; consequently, it must be explained by some attribute, from which, however, it is not distinct except in reason. Therefore, I cannot sufficiently marvel at the subtle ingenuity of those who have sought—not without great detriment to the truth—a mean between being and nothing. But I shall not linger in refutation of their error, seeing that they themselves, when they labor to give definitions of such affections, vanish straightway into the void through their vain subtlety.

2. *Definition of affections.* Let us therefore address our own subject and say that *the affections of being are certain attributes under which we understand the essence or existence of each thing, and from which, however, the affections are distinct only in reason.* Several of these affections of being I shall attempt to explain here (for I do not undertake to handle all of them) and to separate them from denominations which are affections of no being. And first I shall speak of that which is necessary or impossible.

3. *In how many ways a thing is called "necessary" or "impossible."* A thing is called necessary or impossible in two ways: either in respect of its essence or in respect of its cause. In respect of essence we know that God exists necessarily, for his essence cannot be conceived without existence; a chimera, on

the other hand, in respect of its own contradictory essence is not capable of existence. In respect of cause, things, say material things, are called impossible or necessary, for if we regard only their essence, we can conceive it clearly and distinctly without thinking of their existence. For this reason they can never exist through the force and necessity of their essence but only through the force of a cause—for instance, God, creator of all things. And so if it is the divine decree that a particular thing should exist, it necessarily exists; if not, it will be impossible that it should exist. For it is manifestly impossible that a thing should exist which has no internal or external cause of existence. But the material thing assumed in this second hypothesis is such that it cannot exist by the force of its own essence, which is what I mean by an internal cause, nor by the force of divine decree, the unique, external cause of all things; it follows then that it is impossible that the things assumed in the hypothesis should exist.

4. *A chimera can fittingly be called a "verbal entity."* Accordingly, it can be noted first that a chimera can fittingly be called a "verbal entity," since it exists neither in intellect nor in imagination, for it cannot be expressed except by words. For example, through words we can speak of a square circle, but we are unable to imagine it in any way, much less understand it. For this reason a chimera is no more than a word, and as an impossibility it cannot be numbered among the affections of being, for it is mere negation.

5. *Created things depend on God in essence and existence.* Secondly, it should be observed that not only the existence of created things but also their essence and nature depend solely on the decree of God, as we shall fully demonstrate in Part Two below. From this it clearly follows that created things have no necessity of themselves, since they have no essence of themselves and do not exist by themselves.

6. *The necessity which exists in created things through a cause is either of essence or existence; but these are not distinct in God.* Thirdly, and finally, it is to be noted that the sort of necessity which exists in created things through the force of a

cause may be asserted either in respect of their essence or of their existence, for these aspects are distinct in created things. Essence depends upon the eternal laws of nature, but existence upon the series and order of causes. But in God, whose essence is not distinct from his existence, necessity of essence is not distinct from necessity of existence; and from this it follows that if we should think of the whole order of nature, we would find that many things whose nature we clearly and distinctly perceive—that is, whose essence is necessarily such as it is—can in no way exist; for we would discover it to be as impossible for some things of this sort to exist in nature as we know it is for an elephant to pass through the eye of a needle, although we clearly perceive the nature of both the elephant and the needle. Thus, the existence of these things would be only a chimera which we could neither imagine nor understand.

7. *Possibility and contingency are not affections of things.* So much concerning necessity and impossibility. To this it seemed proper to add a little concerning possibility and contingency; for these are sometimes regarded as affections of things, although, on the contrary, they are only defects of our understanding. This I will clearly show after I have explained what is to be understood by these two terms.

8. *What it means to call a thing possible or contingent.* A thing is called possible when we know its efficient cause, and yet do not know whether its cause has been determined. Accordingly, we can consider the thing possible, but neither necessary nor impossible. If, however, we consider only the essence of the thing and not its cause, we shall call it contingent; that is, we shall consider it, so to speak, as a mean between God and a chimera, since on the part of its essence we find in the thing no necessity of existence similar to the necessity in the divine essence, nor do we find the contradiction or impossibility of a chimera. But if anyone wants to call contingent what I call possible, and possible what I call contingent, I shall not contradict him, for I am not used to dispute about words. It will be enough if he grants that these are defects in our perception and nothing real.

9. *Possibility and contingency are simply defects of our understanding.* If anyone wants to deny this, his error can be demonstrated to him with little difficulty. For if he attends to nature and how it depends on God, he will find nothing contingent in things; that is, viewed realistically, he will find nothing in a thing which can exist or not exist, or which, as it is commonly put, is really contingent. This readily appears from what we have shown in Axiom Ten, Part One, namely, that as much force is required to keep a thing in existence as was required to create it. Therefore, no created thing does anything through its own force, just as no created thing begins to exist through its own force. From this it follows that nothing comes into being except through the force of a cause creative of everything, namely, God, who by his concursus at every moment creates everything anew. Since, however, nothing happens save through divine power alone, it is easy to see that things that happen do happen through the force of God's decree and will.[6] But since in God there is no inconstancy or change (by Proposition XVIII and the Corollary of Proposition XX, Part I), the things which he now produces he must have decreed from all eternity he would produce; and since nothing more is necessary for existence than that God has decreed a thing should exist, it follows that in all created things the necessity of existing has existed from eternity. And

[6] [In the Dutch translation of 1664, there is here the following addition: To understand this demonstration well it is necessary to consider with care the discussion of the will of God in the last part of this Appendix. We know the will of God, or his immutable decree, only when we conceive things clearly and distinctly; for the essence of a thing, considered in itself, is nothing but the decree of God or his determinate will. However, we say further that the necessity of real existence is not to be distinguished from the necessity of essence (Part II, Chap. IX); in saying that God has decreed that a triangle should exist, we mean just this, that God has so established the order of nature and its causes that at some determinate moment the triangle must necessarily exist; and, consequently, if we come to know the order of causes as it has been established by God, we will find that it is just as necessary that the triangle really come into existence at some particular moment as it is now necessary, when we consider the nature of a triangle, that its three angles must be equal to two right angles.]

we cannot say that things are contingent because God could have decreed other than he did; for since in eternity there is no when, nor before, nor after, and indeed no relation of time at all, it follows that God never existed before his own decrees so as to have been able to decree other than he did.

10. *To reconcile our freedom of choice with God's predestination exceeds human grasp.* The fact that contingency must be attributed to defects in our understanding pertains also to the freedom of human will, which, in the Scholium to Proposition XV, Part One, we called free; for human will, too, is conserved by the concursus of God and no man wills or does anything except what God has from eternity decreed he should will and do. How this can be, while human freedom is preserved, exceeds our grasp; yet what we clearly perceive is not to be rejected because of that of which we are ignorant. We do clearly and distinctly understand, if we consider our own nature closely, that we are free in our actions and deliberate about many things solely because we want to; if we also attend to the nature of God, we clearly and distinctly perceive, as we have just shown, that everything depends on him and that nothing exists except what has been decreed by God from all eternity to exist. Yet how the human will is created by God in its separate impulses in such a way that it remains free—of this we are ignorant. Actually, there are many things which exceed our grasp, and still we know that they were made by God: for example, the real division of matter into particles indefinite in number, as demonstrated by us in Part Two, Proposition XI, with sufficient evidence, although we are ignorant how that division comes about. Notice that we assume here as a matter of knowledge that the two notions, possible and contingent, signify only a defect of our thought with respect to the existence of a thing.

CHAPTER IV

OF DURATION AND TIME

From the fact that we have divided being into being whose essence involves existence and into being whose essence does not involve existence except as possible, there arises a distinction between eternity and duration. Of eternity we shall speak more fully below.

1. *What eternity is.* Here we simply observe that eternity is an attribute under which we conceive the infinite existence of God.

2. *What duration is.* Duration is an attribute under which we conceive the existence of created things according as they endure in their own actuality. From this it clearly follows that duration is not to be distinguished from the complete existence of a particular thing except in thought. For as the duration of a thing diminishes, its existence also necessarily diminishes. To determine duration, we compare the duration of one thing with the duration of others which have a fixed and determinate motion, and this comparison is called "time."

3. *What time is.* Thus time is not an affection of things but rather a mode of thought or, as we have said, a logical being; for it is a mode of thought serving to explain duration. One should notice here, regarding duration, something which will be useful later when we speak of eternity: that duration is regarded as greater or less, as though composed of parts, and also that it is attributed only to existence and not to essence.

CHAPTER V

CONCERNING OPPOSITION, ORDER, AND SO FORTH

1. *What opposition, order, agreement, diversity, subject, adjunct, and so forth, are.* From the fact that we compare things with one another, there arise certain notions which apart from

things themselves are only modes of thinking. This appears from the fact that if we should regard them as things placed outside thought, we would at once reduce to confusion the clear concept we otherwise had of them. We refer to notions such as opposition, order, agreement, diversity, subject, adjunct, and whatever others there are like them. We perceive such things clearly enough when we think of them only as modes of thinking by which we more easily retain or imagine the things themselves, and not as anything different from the essences of things opposed, ordered, and so forth. Therefore, I do not judge it necessary to discuss them more fully, but pass on to the terms commonly called "transcendental."

CHAPTER VI

OF THE ONE, THE TRUE, AND THE GOOD

These terms are taken by nearly all metaphysicians as the most general affections of being; for they say that all being is one, true, and good, even if no one thinks of such affections. But we shall see what is to be understood by these terms when we have examined each in turn.

1. *What unity is.* And so let us begin with the first, namely, the one. Some say that this term signifies something real, external to the intellect; but what further it adds to being they do not know how to explain, which sufficiently shows that they confuse logical beings with real being and thus succeed in reducing to confusion something they clearly understand. We say, however, that unity is in no way to be distinguished from the thing itself, and that it adds nothing to being; it is rather only a mode of thinking by which we separate one thing from others that are similar to it or in some way agree with it.

2. *What plurality is, and in what sense God can be called "one," and in what sense "unique."* But to unity is opposed plurality, which obviously adds nothing to things and, as we clearly and distinctly understand, is not anything except a mode of thinking. Nor do I see why a clear matter need be

more fully discussed. Here it should only be noted that God, when we set him apart from all other beings, can be called "one"; but when we think that there cannot be several beings having a nature identical with his, he can be called "unique." But yet if we wanted to examine the matter more accurately, we could perhaps show that it is improper to call God "one" and "unique"; however, the matter is of no importance and indeed of no force at all to those who are concerned with things rather than words. So, setting this aside, we pass on to the second term, and in the same passage we will discuss what the term *false* means.

3. *What true and false mean, both in common use and among the philosophers.* That we may rightly perceive these two things, the true and the false, we shall begin with the meaning of the words, from which it will appear that they are only extrinsic classifications of things and are attributed to things only rhetorically. But since common use first discovered these words, which were only afterwards used by the philosophers, it seems pertinent for anyone who inquires into the first meaning of a word to see what it first denoted in common use, especially in the absence of other causes which might be drawn from the nature of language for the purposes of the investigation. The first meaning of true and false seems to have had its origin in narratives; a narrative was called true when it related a fact which had really occurred, and false when it related a fact which had nowhere occurred. Later, the philosophers used this to denote the agreement, and disagreement, of an idea with its object. For this reason an idea is said to be true which presents a thing as it is in itself; but false, which presents a thing to us other than it really is. For ideas are nothing other than narratives or mental histories of nature. Later, the notion was transferred metaphorically to mute things: for example, we call gold true or false, as though gold could be summoned to tell us about itself, whether something is or is not in it.

4. *"True" is not a transcendental term.* Thus, people who judge that "true" is a transcendental term or an affection of

being have plainly been deceived. For it can be asserted of things only improperly or, if you prefer, rhetorically.

5. *How truth and a true idea differ*. If you should ask further what truth is apart from a true idea, ask also what whiteness is apart from a white body, since they are related to one another in the same way.

We have already discussed the cause of the true and the cause of the false, and so there remains nothing to be said here. And even what we have said would not have been worth the trouble if other writers had not so involved themselves in trifles of this sort that they could not extricate themselves, as if they looked for knots in a bulrush.

6. *What the properties of truth are. Certitude is not in things*. The properties of truth or of a true idea are (1) that it be clear and distinct, and (2) that it remove all doubt or, in a word, that it be certain. Those who try to find certitude in things are deceived in the same way as when they look for truth in things. Although we often say that a thing is uncertain, in doing so we take the object of the idea rhetorically for the idea itself. We also do this when we call a thing doubtful, except perhaps in this case we use *uncertainty* in the sense of *contingency*, or we signify a thing which fills us with uncertainty or doubt. There is no need to delay longer over this, so we will go on to the third term and explain at the same time what is meant by its opposite.

7. *Good and evil are predicated only relatively*. A thing is not called good or evil considered in itself, but only in relation to something else to which it contributes in acquiring, or not acquiring, what one loves. Consequently, each and every thing can at the same time under a different aspect be called good and evil. So, for example, the counsel of Ahithophel to Absalom is called good in Holy Scripture; [7] but it was as bad as could be for David, whose death was intended. Indeed, there are many other things which are good, but not for all: thus, salvation [*salus*] is good for men, but is neither good nor bad

[7] [II Sam. 17-18.]

for brutes and plants, since it does not concern them. God, of course, is called utterly good, since he benefits all by conserving through his concursus the being of each and every one—and nothing is more lovable than this. But there is no absolute evil, as is manifest in itself.

8. *Why some have insisted upon a metaphysical good.* Those who keep searching for some metaphysical good, free from relativity, labor under a false prejudice; they confuse a distinction of reason with a real or modal distinction. For they distinguish between a thing itself and the tendency [*conatus*] which is in it to conserve its own being, although they do not know what they mean by this tendency. What very greatly deceives people is that a thing and its tendency to conserve itself, although distinguishable in thought or, more properly, in words, are not distinct from one another in the thing itself.

9. *How a thing and the tendency by which it tries to persevere in its own state are distinguished.* That this may be clearly understood we adduce an example of the simplest sort. Motion has a force for continuing in its own state; this force, obviously, is nothing other than the motion itself: that is, what the nature of motion as such is. For if I say that there is in a body *A* nothing more than a certain quantity of motion, from this it clearly follows, so long as I attend to *A,* that I must always say that this body is moved. If, then, I should say that this body loses through itself its own force of movement, I necessarily attribute something else to it—beyond what we supposed in the hypothesis—through which it loses its own nature. But if this reason seems somewhat obscure, let us concede that this tendency of self-moving is something outside the laws and nature of motion; then since you suppose that this tendency is a metaphysical good, the tendency will also necessarily have a tendency to preserve its being, and this in turn another, and so to infinity, and I know of nothing more absurd. But the reason that they distinguish the tendency of a thing from the thing itself is that they discover in themselves the desire to preserve themselves and they imagine this to be in each and every thing.

10. *Whether God can be called good before he created things.* Still it is asked whether God before he created things could be called good, and from our definition it seems to follow that God did not possess such an attribute, since we say that if a thing is considered solely in itself it cannot be called either good or bad. Now, many will find this absurd, but for what reason I cannot say: for we attribute to God many attributes of this sort which, before things were created, did not belong to him except potentially, as when he is called creator, judge, merciful, and so forth. Such arguments, then, should not delay us.

11. *How perfection is used relatively and how absolutely.* Moreover, just as good and evil are used only relatively, so also with perfection, except when we take perfection for the very essence of a thing; in this sense, as we mentioned before, God possesses infinite perfection—that is, infinite essence or infinite being.

It is not my intention to add to what I have said; for I suppose that whatever else relates to the general part of metaphysics is sufficiently known and is not worth pursuing further.

PART TWO

In which the principal topics concerning God and his Attributes, and human Minds, which commonly occur in special Metaphysics, are briefly explained.[1]

CHAPTER I

OF THE ETERNITY OF GOD

1. *Division of substances.* We have already shown that only substances and their modes exist in nature; thus no one should expect us to say anything here of substantial forms and real accidents, for these things and others of the sort are plainly inept. Next we divided substances into two *summa genera:* namely, extension and thought. Then we divided thought into created thought, that is, human mind, and uncreated, that is, God. The existence of God we have sufficiently demonstrated above, both a posteriori from the idea we have of him, and a priori from his essence, taken as the cause of his existence. But since we treated some of his attributes more briefly than the dignity of the subject requires, we have decided here to take them up again, explaining them at greater length, and at the same time to unravel certain other questions.

2. *Duration does not pertain to God.* The outstanding attribute which must be considered before all the rest is the

1 [In the Dutch translation of 1664, there is here the following addition: In this part, the existence of God is explained quite differently from the manner in which men ordinarily understand it, because they confuse the existence of God with their own, and thus imagine that God is somewhat like a man, not considering the true idea of God which is in them, or ignoring completely that they possess it. Consequently, they are unable to demonstrate the existence of God, either a priori, that is, by the true definition of his essence, or a posteriori, that is, insofar as they possess the idea of him; and thus they can no longer conceive the divine essence. In this part, then, we will attempt to show as clearly as possible that the existence of God is entirely different from that of created things.]

eternity of God, by which we explain his duration; or rather, since we do not attribute duration to God, we say that he is eternal. For as we noted in Part One, duration is an affection of the existence of things and not of their essence; but we cannot attribute duration to God, whose existence belongs to his essence. Those who do attribute duration to God separate his existence from his essence. Indeed, there are those who ask whether God has existed any longer now than at the time when he created Adam; and since this seems sufficiently clear to them, they accordingly decide that duration must in no way be removed from God. Truly, such people beg the question, because they suppose that the essence of God is distinct from his existence. For they ask whether God, who existed up to the time of Adam, has not from the time of Adam's creation until now added additional time to his existence. On this basis, they attribute to God a duration increased by each passing day, and suppose that he is, as it were, continually created by himself. If they did not distinguish the existence of God from his essence, they would not attribute duration to him, since duration absolutely cannot pertain to the essence of things. Surely, no one will ever say that the essence of a circle or triangle, as an eternal truth, has endured longer now than in the time of Adam. Moreover, since duration is thought of as greater and less, as though it consisted of parts, clearly it follows that no duration can be attributed to God: for since his being is eternal—that is, since there can be in it nothing of before or after—we can never attribute duration to it without at the same time destroying the true concept we have of God, since by attributing duration to the being of God we divide into parts that which is infinite in its own nature and which can never be thought of except as infinite.

3. *Why some authors have attributed duration to God.* Some writers have fallen into this error: (1) because they have attempted to explain eternity while not directing their attention to God, as if eternity could be undersood without contemplating the divine essence or as if it were anything but the divine essence. This in turn had its origin in our being

accustomed through the defect of words to attribute eternity
even to things whose essence is distinct from their existence,
as when we say it does not follow that the world has existed
from eternity. We also attribute eternity to the essences of
things so long as we think of them as not existing, for then
we call these essences eternal. (2) Because they did not attribute duration to things except so far as they judged them
to be subject to continual change, and not, as we do, according as their essence is distinct from their existence. (3) Finally,
because they have distinguished the essence of God from his
existence in precisely the same way as in creatures. These errors, I say, have been the occasion of their going astray. For
the first error was responsible for their not understanding
what eternity is, and they have considered it instead as some
species of duration. The second, for their inability to discover
the difference between the duration of created things and the
eternity of God. And the last, for their attributing duration
to God, as we have said; for although duration is only an affection of existence, they distinguished the existence of God
from his essence.

4. *What eternity is.* To understand better what eternity is
and how it cannot be conceived without the divine essence, we
must consider again what we have said before, namely, that
created things, or everything except God, always exist solely
through the force or essence of God and not through their own
force; consequently, only the immutability of God, not the
present existence of things, is the cause of their future existence, and this is why we are compelled to say that whenever
God has once created a thing, he will afterwards keep it in
existence, that is, he will continue the very same act of creating. From this we conclude: (1) that a created thing can be
said to enjoy existence, since existence is not comprised in its
essence, whereas God cannot be said to enjoy existence, for
the existence of God is God himself, and so is his essence. Consequently, created things enjoy duration, but God does not.
(2) All created things, while enjoying their present duration
and existence, are entirely devoid of future existence, since,

obviously, future existence must be given to them continually; but of their essence nothing like this can be said. To God, however, we cannot attribute a future existence since his existence is comprised in his essence; for the very existence he would then have must even now be actually attributed to him; or, to speak more properly, an actually infinite existence belongs to God just as an actually infinite intellect does. This infinite existence I call eternity, and it must be attributed to God alone and not to any created thing, even if its duration is unlimited in the past or in the future. So much of eternity. Of the necessity of God I say nothing, there being no need, since we have demonstrated his existence from his essence. And so we go on to unity.

CHAPTER II

OF THE UNITY OF GOD

We have often marveled at the futile arguments which some writers use to establish the unity of God, arguments such as these: If one God could create a world, all other gods would be useless; and, if all things conspire toward the same end, they have been produced by one maker—and similar arguments taken from extrinsic relations or denominations. And so, setting all these arguments aside, we shall propose here as clearly and as briefly as we can our own demonstration, in the following manner.

God is unique. Among the attributes of God we have numbered the highest possible degree of understanding, and we have said further that he possesses all his perfection from himself and not from another. If you should now say that there are many gods, or beings in the highest degree perfect, all of them must necessarily be supremely intelligent. That this should be, it is not enough that each should understand himself alone; for clearly, since each ought to understand everything, he will have to understand both himself and the others; consequently, the perfection of each one's understanding would depend partly on himself and partly on another. Therefore, no one of them will be able to be a being in the highest degree perfect: that is, as we just noted, a being which takes its entire perfection from itself and not from another. We have already demonstrated, however, that God is a being absolutely perfect and that he exists. Thus, we can now conclude that he exists uniquely; for if several gods were to exist it would follow that the most perfect being possesses imperfection, which is absurd. So much concerning the unity of God.[2]

CHAPTER III

OF THE IMMENSITY OF GOD

1. *In what sense God is called infinite, and in what sense immense.* We have already shown that no being can be thought of as finite and imperfect, or as participating in nothing, except as we first direct our mind to a being perfect and infinite, namely, to God. Therefore, God alone should be called absolutely infinite, so far as we discover that he really consists in infinite perfection. But he can also be called immense, or without limit, so far as we consider that no being exists by which the perfection of God can be limited. From this it follows that the infinity of God, despite the form of the word, is something utterly positive, for we call him infinite so long as we direct our minds to his essence or utmost perfection. But immensity is attributed to God only relatively; for it does not pertain to God as absolutely perfect being, but so far as he is considered the first cause which, although it might not be fully perfect except in respect of second causes, nonetheless would be boundless. For there would be no being more perfect than the first cause, and for this reason no being could be

[2] [The Dutch translation of 1664 has the following addition:
Although this proof can convince us of the unity of God, it cannot explain it. Thus I advise the reader that we should derive the unity of God from the nature of his existence—an existence which is not to be distinguished from his essence and which follows from his essence necessarily.]

thought of by which the first cause could be limited or measured. (For a fuller development of this see Axiom 9, Part I.)

2. *What is commonly meant by the immensity of God.* Some
writers, however, when they treat of the immensity of God,
seem occasionally to attribute quantity to God. For they want
to conclude from this attribute that God must necessarily be
present everywhere, as if they intended to say: If God were not
to exist in some particular place, his quantity would be
limited. The same thing appears somewhat more clearly from
a different argument they use to show that God is infinite or
immense (for they confuse the two terms), and also that he is
everywhere. If God, they say, is pure act, as he certainly is, he
is necessarily everywhere and infinite; for, if he were not everywhere, then either he could not be wherever he wished to be,
or necessarily (*notice this*) he would have to be moved. Thus
it is clear that they attribute immensity to God so far as they
consider him like a quantity, since they take these arguments
of theirs from the properties of extension in order to affirm the
immensity of God, and nothing is more absurd.

3. *The proof that God is everywhere.* If now you ask on
what grounds we will prove that God is everywhere, I reply
that it was already demonstrated sufficiently, and more than
sufficiently, when we showed above that nothing can exist, not
even for a moment, without being created anew by God at
every instant.

4. *The omnipresence of God cannot be explained.* In order
to understand the ubiquity of God, or his presence in things
individually,[3] it would be necessary to penetrate the intimate
nature of the divine will, through which God created things
and continually creates them anew; but since this exceeds human capacity it is impossible to explain how God is everywhere.

3 [Here the Dutch translation inserts the following addition:
It should be observed here that the vulgar make of God a kind of spec-
tator at a theater, when they say that he is everywhere. As we shall
maintain at the end of this part, one sees clearly from this that people
completely confuse the divine nature with human nature.]

5. *Some say that the immensity of God is threefold, but they speak improperly.* Some maintain that the immensity of God is threefold, namely, the immensity of his essence, of his power, and of his presence; but they deal in trifles, because they apparently distinguish between God's essence and his power.

6. *The power of God is not distinct from his essence.* Others have said the same thing more openly, when they affirm that God is everywhere through his power but not through his essence, as if the power of God may be distinguished from all his attributes or from his infinite essence, when in fact it cannot be anything else. For if his power were something else, either it would be some creature, or else some accident, apart from which the divine essence could be conceived. Both these views are absurd. For if it were some creature, it would need the power of God to be kept in existence, and thus an infinite regress is involved. If it were some accident, God would not be a being entirely simple, contrary to what we demonstrated above.

7. *The omnipresence of God is not distinct from his essence.* Finally, by the immensity of his presence they seem, in addition, to intend something other than God's essence, through which things were created and are constantly kept in existence. So great is the absurdity into which they have fallen through confusing God's understanding with man's, and often comparing his power with that of a king!

CHAPTER IV

OF THE IMMUTABILITY OF GOD

1. *The meaning of change, and of transformation.* By change [*mutatio*] we mean here all that variation that can exist in any subject while the essence of the subject remains untouched, although in common use the term is taken more widely to signify the corruption of things—not indeed an absolute corruption, but one which simultaneously entails the generation of something following the corruption, as when we

say that turf changes into dust, or that men turn into beasts. The philosophers, to be sure, denote this by yet another term, namely, transformation [*transformatio*]. But here we speak only of that change in which there is no transformation of the subject, as when we say that Peter changed his color, his habits, and so forth.

2. *Transformation has no place in God.* We must see now whether such changes have a place in God; for there is no need to speak of transformation since we have shown that God exists necessarily, that is, that God cannot cease to be and cannot be transformed into another God; for then he would cease to be and yet at the same time there could be several gods, but we have shown that each of these conjectures is absurd.

3. *What the causes of change are.* To understand more distinctly what remains to be said here, we should consider that every change proceeds either from external causes, whether the subject wills it or not, or from an internal cause, and by the choice of the subject. For example, that a man darkens, becomes ill, grows, and such things, comes about through external causes, sometimes against the subject's will, but sometimes in accordance with his desire; but that he wills, walks, exhibits anger, and so forth, comes about from internal causes.

4. *God is not changed by another.* These changes of the first sort, which come about through external causes, have no place in God, for he is the sole cause of all things and is not acted upon by anyone. Add too the fact that nothing created has in itself any force for existing, and consequently much less the force for performing an action outside itself or of acting upon its own cause. And even if in Sacred Scripture it is often found that God was angered or grieved, and the like, because of men's sins, in these instances the effect is taken for the cause, just as when we say that the sun is stronger or higher in summer than in winter, although it has neither changed its position nor increased its strength. That things such as this are often taught in Holy Scripture is seen in Isaiah, for when he upbraids the people, in chapter 59, verse 2, he says, "But your iniquities have separated between you and your God."

5. *Nor is God changed by himself*. And so we go on to inquire whether there could be in God any change effected by God himself. This we cannot allow to take place in God; on the contrary, we utterly deny it, for all change that depends on will is effected to bring the subject himself to a better condition, a thing which can have no place in a being entirely perfect. Also, such change is not brought about except to avoid some disadvantage or to acquire some good which is lacking, neither of which can have any place in God. We conclude, therefore, that God is an immutable being.[4]

Notice here that I have deliberately omitted the usual divisions of change, although indirectly I have included them too; for there was no need to remove from God, one by one, every kind of change, because in Proposition XVI, Part One, we demonstrated that God is incorporeal, while these common divisions include only changes in matter.

CHAPTER V

OF THE SIMPLICITY OF GOD

1. *Threefold distinction of things: real, modal, and the distinction in reason*. Let us proceed to the simplicity of God. That this attribute of God may be rightly understood, one should recall the matters which Descartes treated in Principles 48 and 49, Part One of the *Principles of Philosophy*, namely, that there is nothing in the nature of things but substances

---

4 [The Dutch translation of 1664 makes the following addition:
One will observe that this is seen much more clearly if one takes account of the nature of the will of God and of his decree. Actually, as will be shown in what follows, the will of God by which he has created things does not differ from his understanding by which he knows them. It is entirely one and the same thing to say that God knows that the three angles of a triangle are equal to two right angles, and to say that God has willed or decreed that the three angles of a triangle should be equal to two right angles; consequently, for us it must be as impossible to conceive that God could change his decrees as it is to think that the three angles of a triangle are not equal to two right angles. Besides, that there could not be any change in God can be demonstrated in other ways, but in order not to be excessively long, we will not do so here.]

and their modes. From this principle there is deduced in Principles 60, 61, and 62 the threefold distinctions of things: real, modal, and the distinction in reason. That distinction is called "real" by which two substances, whether of a diverse or similar attribute, are distinguished from one another: for example, thought and extension, or the parts of matter. And this is known from the fact that each of the two substances can be thought of and, consequently, can exist without the help of the other. The modal distinction is shown to be double: as the distinction which exists between a mode of a substance and the substance itself, and as that which exists between two modes of one and the same substance. The latter we know from the fact that although each mode may be thought of without the aid of the other, yet neither can be thought of without the help of the substance of which they are modes. The former is known from the fact that although the substance can be thought of without its mode, still the mode cannot be thought of without its substance. A distinction in reason, finally, is that which occurs between a substance and its own attribute, as when duration is distinguished from extension. And this distinction is known from the fact that a substance of a particular sort cannot be understood without its particular attribute.

3. *God is an entirely simple being.* Now it must be shown that God is not a composite being; from this we will be able to conclude that he is an entirely simple being, and this we will do easily. For since it is self-evident that the parts which compose a thing are prior, in nature at least, to the thing which they compose, necessarily those substances from whose coalition and union God would be composed will be prior in nature to God himself, and each will be able to be conceived through itself, without being attributed to God. Then, since these substances should necessarily be really distinct from one another, necessarily each could exist through itself and without the help of the others, so that, as we have just said, there could be as many gods as there are substances of which God

is supposed to be composed. For each, being able to exist through itself, will have to exist from itself; consequently, it will have the power of giving to itself all the perfections which we have shown are in God, as we have already explained at length in Proposition VII, Part One, where we demonstrated the existence of God. Since, however, nothing can be more absurd than this, we conclude that God is not composed of a coalition and union of substances. Again, that there is in God no composition of diverse modes is sufficiently evident from the fact that there are no modes in God, since modes arise from an alteration of substance. (See *Principles of Philosophy,* Part I, Principle 56.) Finally, if anyone should wish to imagine another sort of composition formed from the essence of things and their existence, we would not oppose him. But let him remember that we have already demonstrated that essence and existence are not distinct in God.

4. *The attributes of God are distinct only in reason.* Now we can clearly conclude that all the distinctions we make among the attributes of God are only distinctions in reason, and that these attributes are not actually separated from one another. One must understand by distinctions in reason such distinctions as I have just discussed, namely, those which are known from the fact that a substance of a certain sort cannot exist without its particular attribute. From this we conclude that God is an entirely simple being. Since we are not concerned with the hodgepodge of distinctions made by the Peripatetics, we pass on to the life of God.

CHAPTER VI

OF THE LIFE OF GOD

1. *What philosophers commonly mean by life.* To understand correctly this attribute, namely, the life of God, we must explain in general what is denoted in each thing by its life. First we will examine the opinion of the Peripatetics. By life

they understood *the indwelling of a nutritive soul accompanied by heat.* (See Aristotle, *de Respiratione* 8.[5]) Since they have imagined three souls—vegetative, sensitive, and intellectual—which they attribute only to plants, to animals, and to men, it follows, as they themselves confess, that other beings have no share in life. But meanwhile they would not dare say that minds [*mentes*] and God lack life, perhaps for fear of falling into the contrary assertion: namely, that if they lack life, they have died. This is why Aristotle in the *Metaphysics,* Book Eleven, Chapter 7,[6] gives still another definition of life, peculiar to minds only: *actuality of thought is life,* and in this sense he attributes life to God as a being who understands and is pure act. But we shall not take many pains to refute this, for, as we have already demonstrated, these three souls which they attribute to plants, animals, and men are nothing but figments, since we have shown that nothing exists in matter other than mechanical structures and operations. However, in respect of the life of God, I do not see why Aristotle should mention the act of thought rather than the act of will or some other faculty. But since I expect no reply to this, I pass on to explain, as we promised, what life is.

2. *To what things life can be attributed.* Although this word is often extended metaphorically to signify the customs of a particular man, we will explain only what it means philosophically. It should be noted, however, that if life must also be attributed to corporeal things, nothing will lack a share in it; but if it should be attributed only to things in which a soul is united to a body, then it will have to be attributed only to men, or perhaps to animals, but not to minds [*mentibus*] and not to God. But since the word *life* is commonly applied rather widely, doubtless it must be attributed to corporeal things not united to minds, and to minds separated from bodies.

3. *What life is; and what it is in God.* Therefore, by life we understand a force through which things persevere in their

5 [Aristotle, *de Respiratione* 8, 474a25-30.]

6 [Spinoza has cited the reference incorrectly. *Metaphysics* XII. 8, 1072b25.]

own being. Since this force is distinct from the things themselves, we may properly say that things have life. But the force
by which God perseveres in his being is nothing but his essence. Consequently, they speak very well who call God "Life."
There are some theologians who understand that it is for this
reason—because God is life and is not distinguished from life—
that the Jews, on taking an oath, bespoke *the living Jehovah*
and not *the life of Jehovah,* whereas Joseph bespoke *the life of
Pharaoh* when he swore by the life of Pharaoh.

CHAPTER VII

OF THE UNDERSTANDING OF GOD [7]

1. *God is omniscient.* Among the attributes of God we have
included heretofore omniscience, which obviously belongs to
God, since knowledge entails perfection, and since God as a
being entirely perfect lacks no perfection. Consequently, knowledge must be attributed to God in its highest degree, knowledge which does not presuppose or imply any ignorance or
privation, otherwise there would be imperfection in that attribute, and in God. From this it follows that God's understand-

[7] [In the Dutch translation of 1664, the following is inserted as the first
paragraph of this chapter:
In the three following chapters we will treat the understanding of God,
his will, and his power, and we will be able to conclude quite clearly
from them that the essences of things and the necessity of their existence,
beginning with a given cause, are all nothing other than the will or
decree of God. This is why the will of God appears to us most clearly
when we conceive things clearly and distinctly. Indeed, it is laughable
that the philosophers, when they are ignorant of causes, attempt to take
refuge in the divine will, as one often sees. For, they say, things whose
causes are unknown to us are produced entirely by God's good will and
his absolute decree. The common philosophy has not found a better
proof of the divine providence and design than one based upon ignorance of causes. It is clear that the common philosophy is absolutely ignorant of the divine nature, and attributes to it a will similar to that of
man, which, in us, is conceived as distinct from the understanding. I
believe that there is to be seen in this the sole basis of superstition and
of numerous evils.]

ing was never potential, and that he does not come to conclusions by discursive reasoning.

2. *The object of God's knowledge is not anything external
to God.* Moreover, it follows from the perfection of God that
his ideas are not determined as ours are by external objects.
On the contrary, things created by God external to himself are
determined by his understanding,[8] otherwise such objects
would possess their nature and essence through themselves and,
in nature at least, would be prior to the divine intellect; and
this is absurd. By not observing this with sufficient care, people
have fallen into enormous errors. Some indeed have asserted
that apart from God there exists matter, coeternal with him
and self-existent; and that, according to some, God in his
understanding has only reduced this matter to order, while,
according to others, he has also impressed forms upon it. Still
others have asserted that things are by their own nature either
necessary, or impossible, or contingent, and, consequently,
that God knows them as contingent and is utterly ignorant
whether they exist or not. Then others have said that God
knows contingent things through their circumstances, perhaps
because he has had extensive experience. Beyond these I could
cite still other such errors, if I did not judge it to be useless,
since their falsity is immediately obvious from what has already been said.

3. *The object of God's knowledge is God himself.* Let us return to our own proposition, that no object of God's knowledge exists outside God, but that he is himself the object of his
own knowledge and, indeed, is his own knowledge. Those who
think that the universe, at least, is the object of God's knowledge see no further into the matter than those who would say
that the object of a distinguished architect's knowledge is some
building he has made. For a workman is still compelled to look
for suitable material outside himself; yet God seeks no material
external to himself; on the contrary, things, in both their es-

8 Hence it clearly follows that the intellect by which God understands
created things, and the will and power by which he has determined them,
are one and the same thing.

sence and existence, have been fabricated by his intellect or will.

4. *How God knows sins, being of reason, and so forth.* The question arises whether God knows evils or sins, beings of reason, and such things. We answer that God must necessarily understand things of which he is the cause, especially since they could not exist even for a moment without the divine concursus. Yet, since evils and sins are nothing in things, but are only in a human mind comparing things with one another, it follows that God does not know them as something external to human minds. We have maintained that beings of reason are modes of thought and in this sense they must be known by God, that is, insofar as we see that he conserves and creates the human mind exactly as it is constituted; but not because God himself has similar modes of thinking for retaining more easily the things he understands. If these few things we have mentioned are properly attended to, nothing can be proposed about the understanding of God which cannot be solved with little trouble.

5. *How God knows individuals and universals.* Meanwhile, we must not ignore the error of those who assert that God knows only eternal things like angels and heavens, which they imagine are self-begotten and incorruptible; while of this world he knows nothing but species, also regarded as self-begotten and incorruptible. Such people seem to want, almost studiously, to be wrong and to cogitate absurdities. For what can be more absurd than to remove from God's knowledge the individual things which cannot exist for a moment without him? Thus they say that God is ignorant of things really existing, but they then attribute to God, in their imagining, a knowledge of universals, which do not exist and have no essence apart from that of individual things. We, on the contrary, attribute to God a knowledge of individual things, but we deny that he has knowledge of universals except as he understands human minds.

6. *There is in God only one simple idea.* Finally, before we end this argument, it seems that a satisfactory answer should

be made to the question whether there are several ideas in God or only a perfectly simple one. To this I reply that the idea of God, through which he is called omniscient, is unique and entirely simple. For obviously God is called omniscient only because he has an idea of himself; this idea or cognition has always existed simultaneously with him, since nothing exists apart from his essence, and this idea could not have existed apart from him.

7. *What God's knowledge of created things is.* But God's understanding of created things cannot with complete propriety be referred to God's knowledge. For if God had so wished, created things might have had a different essence, but this possibility has no place in God's understanding of himself. However proper or improper it may be to call this understanding of created things an understanding, someone will ask whether it is unique or multiple. But, we reply, this question does not differ from those which ask whether God's decrees and volitions are many or not, and whether God's ubiquity, or the concursus by which he sustains individual things, is the same in all. As we have already said, we can have no distinct knowledge of such things. Evidently, however, just as we know that God's concursus must be unique if it is referred to his omnipotence, even though it reveals itself in diverse effects, so also God's volitions and decrees (for so one may call his understanding of created things) considered in God are not multiple, although they have been expressed diversely through or, more properly, in created things. If, then, we consider the analogy of the whole of nature, we can regard it as one being, and consequently God's idea, or judgment, of created nature [*Natura naturata*] will only be one.

CHAPTER VIII

OF THE WILL OF GOD

1. *We do not know how the essence of God, the intellect by which he understands himself, and the will by which he loves*

himself are distinguished. The will of God by which he wills
to love himself follows necessarily from the infinite intellect by
which he understands himself. Yet how these three things are
to be distinguished, namely, God's essence, the intellect by
which he understands himself, and the will by which he wills
to love himself, we leave among things yet to be solved. We
are not unaware of the term (that is, *personality*) which theologians occasionally use to explain the matter; but although
we are not ignorant of the term, we are ignorant of its meaning and can form no clear and distinct concept of it, although
we steadfastly believe that God will reveal it to his own in
the beatific vision which is promised to the faithful.

2. *The will and power of God with respect to external
things are not distinct from his intellect.* The will and power
of God with respect to external things are not distinct from his
intellect, as is sufficiently evident from what has already been
said. For we have shown that God has decreed not only that
things should exist, but that they should exist with a particular
kind of nature; that is, their essence and their existence had to
depend on God's will and power. Thus we clearly and distinctly perceive that the intellect, power, and will by which
God created, understood, and now conserves or loves created
things are not distinct among themselves but only in our
thought.

3. *It is improperly said that God hates or loves certain
things.* When we say that God hates or loves certain things, the
sense is the same as when Scripture records, for example, that
the earth will vomit forth men, and other things of this sort.
That God is not angered at anyone and does not love things
in the way common people suppose may be gathered from
Scripture itself: for Isaiah and, more clearly, the Apostle in
Romans 9, said, "For the children being not yet born [namely,
the children of Isaac], neither having done any good or evil,
that the purpose of God according to the election might stand,
not of works, but of him that calleth; it was said unto her
[Rebecca], The elder shall serve the younger," and so forth.
And a little further on, "Therefore hath he mercy on whom

he will have mercy, and whom he will he hardeneth. Thou wilt say then unto me, Why doth he yet find fault? For who hath resisted his will? Nay but, O man, who art thou that repliest against God? Shall the thing formed say to him that formed it, Why hast thou made me thus? Hath not the potter power over the clay, of the same lump to make one vessel unto honour, and another unto dishonour?" [9]

4. *Why God admonishes men; why he does not save them without admonition; and why the impious are punished.* If you ask why God admonishes men, the answer is easily given: because God has decreed from eternity to admonish men at the appropriate time, in order that those whom he wished saved might be converted. If you then ask whether God could have saved them without that admonition, we answer that he could. Why then does he not save them, you might ask next. I will reply to this after you tell me why God did not make the Red Sea passable without a vehement east wind, and why he did not perfect all individual motions without the help of other motions, and why he performs countless other things through mediate causes. And yet again you will ask, Why then are the impious punished, for they act according to their nature and the divine decree? But, I reply, it is also by the divine decree that they are punished; and if only those should be punished who we suppose sin through their own will alone, why do men try to exterminate poisonous serpents, since they offend only through their own nature and could not do otherwise?

5. *Scripture teaches nothing repugnant to the Light of Nature.* Finally, if there are other things in Sacred Scripture which induce uneasiness, this is not the place to explain them. Here we inquire only into things which we can comprehend with complete certainty through natural reason, and it is enough that we demonstrate such things with sufficient evidence to know that Sacred Scripture ought likewise to teach the same things; for truth does not contradict truth, and Scripture cannot teach such trifles as are commonly supposed.

[9] [Rom. 9:11-12, 18-21.]

For if we should find in Scripture anything contrary to the Natural Light, we could confute Scripture with the same freedom with which we confute the Koran and Talmud. But we are far from thinking that anything could be found in Sacred Literature which is repugnant to the Light of Nature.

CHAPTER IX

OF THE POWER OF GOD

1. *How the omnipotence of God is to be understood.* That God is omnipotent has already been satisfactorily demonstrated. Here we shall only try to explain briefly how this attribute is to be understood, since many speak of it with insufficient piety and not according to the truth. For they say that some things are possible through their own nature and not by the decree of God; that some things are impossible, and others, again, necessary; and that God's omnipotence applies only to the possible. We, however, having already shown that everything depends absolutely upon God's decree, say that God is omnipotent. In addition, having understood that he has decreed some things solely through the freedom of his will, and also that he is immutable, we now say that nothing can act contrary to his decrees, and that such action is impossible solely because it is contrary to the perfection of God.

2. *All things are necessary in virtue of the decree of God; it is not true that some things are necessary in themselves, others in respect of God's decree.* Some will perhaps argue that we find certain things necessary only while we direct our attention to God's decree, whereas we find other things necessary even when we do not attend to God's decree: for example, the fact that Josiah burned the bones of the idolaters on the altars of Jeroboam.[10] For if we consider only Josiah's will, we will look on the matter as possible and will certainly not say that it necessarily had to happen, except insofar as the prophet had predicted it from the decree of God; but that the

10 [II Kings 23:15-18.]

three angles of a triangle should be equal to two right angles is revealed by the very being of the triangle. Such people, however, make distinctions in things out of their own ignorance. For if men clearly understood the whole order of nature, they would find everything just as necessary as the things treated in mathematics; but since this is beyond human understanding, we regard certain things as possible rather than necessary. Thus we must say either that God can do nothing, since all things are obviously necessary, or, that God can do everything, and that the necessity we find in things came solely from God's decree.

3. *If God had made the nature of things other than it is, he would also have had to give us a different intellect.* But it might now be asked, What if God had decreed things other than they are now and had made things false which now are actually true, would we not in that case still take them for true? Certainly, if God had left us with the nature which he has given us; but then, had he so wished, he could have given us a nature capable of understanding the newly ordained nature and laws of things, just as our present nature can understand the present order; indeed, if we consider his veracity, he would have had to do so. This also appears from what we said above, that the whole of created nature exists as a unique being; consequently, man is a part of nature and ought to cohere with the rest. Thus from the simplicity of God's decree it should also follow that had God created things in some different manner, he would at the same time have made our nature capable of understanding things according as he himself had created them. And so, although we want to keep the distinction in God's power which philosophers commonly teach, still we are compelled to explain it differently.

4. *The fourfold division of God's power. What the absolute, the ordaining, the ordinary, and the extraordinary powers of God are.* Accordingly, we divide the power of God into ordaining and absolute. We call God's power absolute when we consider his omnipotence without considering his decrees; but ordaining when we look to his decrees.

Moreover, God's power is both ordinary and extraordinary. The ordinary power of God is that by which he keeps the existence of the universe in a definite order; but his power is extraordinary when he does anything beyond the order of nature, as, for example, all miracles like speech in a donkey, the apparition of angels, and such things. However, this last division can with good reason be doubted, since it would seem more miraculous for God always to govern the universe in one definite and immutable order than to abrogate, for the sake of human folly, the laws which he himself has freely ordained as best in nature (which no one can deny except through deep, intrinsic blindness). But this we leave for the theologians to decide.

Finally, we omit other questions commonly raised with regard to God's power, for instance, whether God's power extends over the past, whether he can do things better than he does, whether he can do more than he has done. From what has been said, it is very easy to reply to these.

CHAPTER X

OF CREATION

We have established heretofore that God is the creator of all things. Here we shall try to explain what is to be understood by creation; and then we will clarify as best we can the things commonly proposed about creation. And so let us start with the first.

1. *What creation is.* Accordingly, we say that creation is an operation in which no causes concur except the efficient cause, that is, a created thing is one which presupposes nothing for its existence except God.

2. *The common definition of creation is rejected.* It would be well to notice, first, that we omit the words *ex nihilo,* commonly used by philosophers, as if *nothing* were a material out of which things were produced. They speak this way because they constantly suppose that when things are being produced

there is something antecedent to them from which they come about, and so, when speaking of creation, they could not omit this particle, *ex.* They do the same thing with matter. Since they see that all bodies exist in a place and are bounded by other bodies, they have asked themselves *where* matter, in its totality, exists, and they have answered: in some imaginary space. Thus, without doubt, rather than considering *nihil* as a negation of all reality, they have supposed or imagined that it is something real.

3. *The proper definition explained.* Secondly, notice my saying that no causes except the efficient concur in creation. Of course, I could have said that creation denies or excludes all causes except the efficient. But I preferred *concur* to avoid being compelled to answer those who ask whether in creation God had any end in view for the sake of which he created things. Also, to explain the matter better, I added a second definition, namely, that a created thing presupposes nothing except God. For if God had some end in mind, certainly it did not exist outside him, since nothing exists external to God by which he may be driven to act.

4. *Accidents and modes are not created.* Thirdly, from this definition it follows that there is no creation of accidents and modes, for they presuppose created substance in addition to God.

5. *Before creation there was no time or duration.* Fourthly, before creation we can imagine no time and no duration; rather, they began with things. For time is the measure of duration, and indeed is nothing but a mode of thinking. Thus, it presupposes not just any sort of created thing, but especially thinking men. Duration, however, ceases when created things cease to exist, and begins when created things begin to exist. I say created things, for only eternity pertains to God, and not duration, as we have shown with sufficient evidence above. Thus, duration presupposes created things or at least implies them. Those, however, who imagine duration and time before created things manifestly labor under the same prejudice as

those who imagine a space external to matter. So much for the definition of creation.

6. *God creates the universe and sustains it by the same act.* Next, there is no need here to repeat again our demonstration in Axiom Ten, Part One, that the same forces are required for creating a thing as for sustaining it: that is, that the operation of God in creating and in conserving the universe is one and the same thing.

Having noted these things, let us go on to the second thing we proposed. Accordingly, we must ask first what has been created and what not created; and second, whether what has been created could have been created from eternity.

7. *The kinds of things that have been created.* To the first we answer briefly that everything has been created whose essence is clearly conceived apart from its existence, and yet is conceived through itself, for example, matter, of which we have a clear and distinct concept when we think of it under the attribute of extension, and which we think of with equal clarity and distinctness whether it exists or not.

8. *How God's thought differs from our own.* Yet some will perhaps maintain that we clearly and distinctly think of thought apart from existence, and yet attribute it to God. The answer to this is that we do not attribute to God a thought similar to our own, subject to passion and limited by the nature of things, but a thought which is pure act, involving existence, as we have demonstrated at sufficient length above. For we have shown that the intellect and will of God are not to be separated from his power and essence, which do involve existence.

9. *There is nothing external to God which is coeternal with him.* Accordingly, since everything whose essence does not entail existence must be created by God in order to exist, and must, as we have shown in many places above, be continually conserved by its creator, we shall not linger to refute the opinion of those who have made the universe, or chaos, or formless matter, coeternal with God and, consequently, independent.

Accordingly, we must go on to the second part and inquire whether what has been created could have been created from eternity.

10. *What is meant here by the phrase, "from eternity."* That this may be rightly understood one should pay attention to the expression, "from eternity," since we want to use it in this part of the discussion with an entirely different meaning from that which it had earlier when we spoke of the eternity of God. For here we take it to mean nothing but duration without a beginning of duration, or a duration which we cannot express by any number however great, even though we try to multiply it by many years or myriads of years and the product again by myriads.

11. *Proof that a thing could not be created from eternity.* That such a duration cannot exist is clearly demonstrable. For if the universe were led backwards through time from the present moment, it could never have had this sort of duration; and so the universe could not have arrived at the present from such a beginning. You will perhaps say that nothing is impossible for God since he is omnipotent, and that consequently he could bring about a duration which could not be exceeded. Now we answer that because God is omnipotent he never will create a duration such that he could not create a still greater one. For such is the nature of duration that it can always be conceived as greater or less than already supposed, just like number. You will perhaps urge that God has existed from eternity and, thus, has endured until now, so that a duration does exist than which a greater cannot be conceived. But this attributes to God a duration consisting of parts, a concept which we sufficiently refuted when we demonstrated that eternity, not duration, pertains to God. How I wish that men had considered this properly; for then they could easily have extricated themselves from many arguments and absurdities, and could have been held with uttermost delight in the beatific contemplation of this being.

But let us go on to reply to the arguments of those who try

to show the possibility of such infinite duration from a point in the past.

12. *From the fact that God is eternal it does not follow that his effects can exist from eternity.* In the first place, they argue that a thing which has been produced can coexist with its cause; but since God has existed from eternity, his effects likewise could have been produced from eternity. And they confirm this moreover by the example of the son of God who has been produced by the father from eternity. Obviously, from what has been said before, they confuse eternity with duration and attribute to God only a duration from eternity, and this also appears from the example they introduce. For they assert that the very same eternity which they attribute to the son of God is possible for creatures. They imagine, then, a time and duration before the foundation of the universe, and they want to assert duration apart from created things just as others have asserted eternity apart from God. It is evident by now that both these views are utterly inconsistent with truth. So we reply that it is absolutely false to say that God can communicate his own eternity to creatures; and that the son of God is not a creature, but just like the father, is eternal. Accordingly, when we say that the father has begotten the son from eternity, we mean nothing other than that the father has always communicated his own eternity to the son.

13. *If God acted by necessity, his virtue would not be infinite.* In the second place they argue that God, when he acts freely, is not of less power than when he acts by necessity; moreover, that if God did act by necessity, since his virtue is infinite, he must have created the world from eternity. But this argument too can be easily met if one attends to its basis. In effect, these good men suppose that they can possess contrary ideas of a being of infinite virtue; for they think that God is of infinite virtue both when he acts by the necessity of his nature and when he acts freely. We, on the contrary, deny that God is of infinite virtue if he acts by the necessity of his nature, and our denial is allowable, indeed must be conceded

by them necessarily, inasmuch as we have demonstrated that an entirely perfect being acts freely and cannot be thought of except as unique. But so far as they insist, however impossible it may actually be, that it is still possible to assume that God is of infinite virtue while acting by the necessity of his nature, we will reply that this is no more allowable than postulating a square circle as the basis for concluding that all the lines drawn from its center to the circumference are not equal. This is sufficiently established from what we said a moment ago, not to mention what we have long been saying. For we have just demonstrated that relative to any duration which actually exists, we can always imagine another twice or half as long; consequently God, who acts freely by infinite virtue, can always create a duration larger or smaller than the one given. But if God were to act by the necessity of his nature this would not follow, since only that duration which would result from his nature could be produced by God, and not countless others greater than the one given. Therefore, our argument briefly is this: If God should create a maximum duration such that even he could not create a greater, he would necessarily diminish his own power. But this would be false, for his power does not differ from his essence. Therefore, and so forth. Besides, if God should act by the necessity of his nature, he would have to create a duration greater than any other he could create; but in creating such a duration God is not of infinite virtue, for we can always think of a duration greater than the one supposed. Therefore, if God acted from the necessity of his nature, he would not be of infinite virtue.

14. *Whence we have the concept of a duration greater than that of the universe.* But if anyone should find difficulty now in understanding from what source we can conceive a duration longer than that of the universe, seeing that the universe, if the computation of chronology be correct, was created somewhat more than five thousand years ago, and since we have asserted that duration cannot be understood apart from created things, the difficulty is easily resolved if one notices that we understand this duration not simply from the contemplation

of created things, but also from contemplation of the infinite creative power of God. For creatures cannot be thought of as existing and enduring through themselves, but only through God's infinite power from which alone they possess their entire duration. (See Proposition XII, Part I, and its Corollary.)

Finally, so as not to waste time here in replying to futile arguments, one should simply attend to the distinction between eternity and duration, and to the fact that duration apart from created things, and eternity apart from God, are not intelligible. Once these are properly perceived, one can easily reply to all arguments, and so we do not think it necessary to dwell any longer upon them.

CHAPTER XI

OF THE CONCURSUS OF GOD

Concerning this attribute little or nothing remains to be said, since we have shown that at every moment God continually creates a thing, as it were, entirely anew; and then we demonstrated that things never have of themselves any power for doing anything or for determining themselves to any action; and this applies not only to things outside men, but also to human will itself. Then, also, we replied to several arguments concerning these things, and although many others are customarily proposed, it is my intention to pass them by since they pertain principally to theology.

However, since there are many who admit and maintain the concursus of God in a sense plainly different from ours, we must notice here, in order to expose their fallacy the more easily, what we have demonstrated hitherto: namely, that present time has no connection with future time (see Axiom 10, Part I), and that we clearly and distinctly perceive this. If this is properly kept in mind, all the arguments which can be drawn from philosophy will be met with no difficulty.

1. *How God's conservation of things is affected in his determining them to act.* However, in order not to have raised

the question of God's concursus uselessly, we shall in passing
answer this question: Is anything added to the action by which
God conserves things, when he determines a thing to act?
When we spoke of motion we had already touched upon the
reply to this. For we said that God keeps unchanged the quantity of motion in nature. Therefore, if we consider the whole
of material nature, nothing new is added to that; but in respect of particular things it can in some sense be said that
something new is added there. Whether this also occurs in
spiritual things is not apparent; for these do not seem to be
so mutually dependent. Next, since the parts of duration have
no mutual connection, we can say that God more properly
precreates things than conserves them; consequently, if a man
now possesses a determinate liberty to do a particular thing, it
must be said that God has created him so at this moment. It
is no objection to this that the human will is often determined
by things placed outside it, and that all the things in nature
are mutually determined by themselves to a particular operation, for they are also determined so by God. Nothing, indeed,
can determine the will, nor in turn can the will be determined,
except by the power of God. But how this is not repugnant to
human liberty or how God can accomplish it while still preserving human liberty, we confess we do not know, as we have
often already said.

2. *The common division of the attributes of God is more
verbal than real.* These, then, are the things I had decided to
mention about the attributes of God, among which, until now,
I have made no division. The division which is often given
by authors, and which consists in dividing the attributes of
God into incommunicable and communicable, seems, I fear,
more the division of a word than of a thing. For the knowledge
of God is no more like human knowledge than Canis, the
celestial dog, is like a dog that barks—indeed, much less.

3. *The author's division.* But we offer the following division.
There are some attributes of God which explain his active essence; others, having nothing to do with his action, which
describe his mode of existing. Of the latter sort are unity,

eternity, necessity, and the like; of the former, intelligence, will, life, omnipotence, and so forth. This division is sufficiently clear and perspicuous and includes all the attributes of God.

CHAPTER XII

OF HUMAN MIND

We must go on now to created substance, which we have divided into extended substance and thinking substance. By extended substance we mean matter or corporeal substance; but by thinking substance, human mind alone.

1. *Angels are a subject for theology, not for metaphysics.* Although angels too have been created, yet, since they are not known by Natural Light, they are not considered in metaphysics. Their essence and existence are known only through revelation, and thus pertain only to theology, the knowledge of which is not to be mixed with natural knowledge, since it is different, indeed generically different, from natural knowledge. No one should expect us, therefore, to say anything about angels.

2. *Human mind does not exist through propagation, but is created by God; yet we do not know when it is created.* So let us return to human minds, of which little remains now to be said; we need only point out that we have said nothing of the time at which the human mind is created, because there is not sufficient proof when God creates it, since it can exist without the body. This much is evident, that it does not exist by propagation, for propagation occurs only in things that are generated, that is, to be precise, in the modes of some substance, while substance itself cannot be generated, but can only be created by omnipotence, as we have demonstrated heretofore.

3. *In what sense the human soul* [anima] *is mortal.* I should add a little about the immortality of the soul. It is evident that we cannot say of any created thing that its nature implies that it may not be destroyed by God. For he who has the power to

create a thing has also the power to destroy it. Consider also, as we have already shown, that no created thing can exist through its own nature even for a moment, but must be continually procreated by God.

4. *In what sense the human soul is immortal.* Still, despite this, we see clearly and distinctly that we have no idea by which we might conceive the destruction of substance similar to the ideas we have of the generation and corruption of modes. For when we consider the structure of the human body, we clearly conceive that such a structure can be destroyed; but when we consider corporeal substance we do not as clearly see that it can be annihilated. Then, too, a philosopher does not inquire into what God can do with his full power, but he judges of the nature of things from the laws which God has imparted to them. Accordingly, he judges that a thing is fixed and certain when he deduces by means of these laws that it is fixed and certain, although he does not deny that God can change these laws and everything else. For this reason, when we speak of the soul we do not ask what God can do, but only what follows from the laws of nature.

5. *The soul's immortality demonstrated.* Since from these considerations it clearly follows that substance cannot be destroyed either by itself or by another created substance, as we have already, I hope, abundantly demonstrated, we are compelled by the laws of nature to assert that the mind [*mentem*] is immortal. And if we cared to consider the matter even more closely, we could demonstrate with perfect assurance that it is immortal. For, as we have just shown, it follows from the laws of nature that the soul [*anima*] is immortal. Now the laws of nature are the decrees of God revealed through the Natural Light, as is also fully established above. Further, we have also demonstrated that the decrees of God are immutable. From all this we clearly conclude that God has disclosed to men his immutable will with regard to the duration of souls not only in revelation but also through the Natural Light.

6. *God does not act against nature, but beyond it; what this means according to the author.* Nor is there any difficulty

should someone object that God sometimes destroys these natural laws in order to effect miracles; for many of the more prudent theologians concede that God does not act against nature but beyond it; that is, as I explain the matter, God has many laws of action which he has not communicated to the human understanding, and which, if they had been communicated, would be as natural as the others.

Thus, it is quite clear that minds are immortal, and I do not see what remains to be said here of the human soul in general. Nor would there be anything to say of its special functions, if the arguments by which certain authors attempt to prove that they do not see and feel what they do see and feel did not induce me to make a reply.

7. *Why some think that the will is not free.* Some think they can show that the will is not free, but is always determined by another. They think this because they understand by will something distinct from the soul, and they regard the will as a substance whose nature consists solely in indifference. However, to remove all confusion we shall first explain the nature of will, and once that is done we shall easily expose their fallacies.

8. *What will is.* We have said that the human mind is a thinking thing; whence it follows that solely from its own nature, considered in itself alone, the mind can do something: it can think—affirm and deny. But its thoughts are determined either by things located outside the mind or by the mind alone; and since it is itself a substance, many mental actions can and should follow from its essence as a thinking thing. Those mental actions, however, which have no other cause than human mind are called "volitions." Now, when the human mind is regarded as the sufficient cause of such actions it is called "will."

9. *Will exists.* The example of Buridan's ass [11] is a conven-

---

11 [To Buridan is attributed the sophism: If a hungry ass were placed exactly between two stacks of hay which were in every respect equal, it would have no motive for preferring one haystack to the other, and would consequently starve to death.]

ient means of explaining that the soul has a power of will even when it is not determined by external things. If a man placed in the same dilemma as Buridan's ass should perish from hunger and thirst, he would be regarded as a stupid ass rather than a thinking thing. Then too, the soul's power of will can also be seen in our willingness, as we have said before, to doubt everything, and to expose as false everything that can be reduced to doubt. (See Descartes' *Principles,* Part I, Principle 39.)

10. *Will is free.* Further, it should be noticed that even if the soul is determined by external things to affirm or deny something, it always remains essentially free because its being determined in this way is not the same as being compelled by external things. For nothing has the power to destroy the soul's essence, and so it always affirms or denies freely whatever it does affirm or deny. This was sufficiently explained in the "Fourth Meditation." Therefore, when asked why the soul wills or does not will this thing or that, we reply: because the soul is a thinking thing, a thing which has by its own nature the power of willing or nilling and of affirming or denying; for this is what it means to be a thinking thing.

11. *Will is not to be confused with appetite.* Having explained these matters, let us look to the arguments of our adversaries. Their first argument is: "If the will can will contrary to the final decision of the intellect, and desire contrary to the good prescribed by the final decision of the intellect, it can desire evil under the aspect of evil. But such a conclusion is absurd, and therefore the premise is also absurd." Clearly, people who offer this argument do not understand what will is; they confuse it with the appetite which the soul possesses after it has affirmed or denied a thing. They have learned this from their master [12] who defined will as *appetitus sub ratione boni.* But we say that will is the affirmation or denial that a thing is good, and we explained the matter profusely while discussing the cause of error, where we demonstrated that error arose because will extends more widely than

[12] [Aristotle. But the language of the definition is scholastic. See, for example, Thomas Aquinas, *Summa Theologica,* I, II, q. 8, a. 1.]

understanding. In fact, if the mind did not affirm that a thing is good, by the very fact that it is free it would desire nothing. Accordingly, in reply to the argument we grant that the mind can will nothing against the final decision of the understanding. More precisely, the will cannot will a thing which we have assumed it does not will. But this principle is presupposed here when we say that the mind has judged a thing to be evil, since this means that the mind has not willed it. Yet we deny that the mind absolutely cannot will a thing which is evil—that is, judge it to be good—since this would be contrary to experience. In fact, we often think things are good when they are evil, or evil when they are good.

12. *Will is nothing but the mind itself*. Their second argument (or, if you prefer, the first, since as yet there has been no argument) is: "If the will is not determined to will by the last judgment of the practical intellect, then it will determine itself. But the will does not determine itself, because it is essentially and by its own nature indeterminate." From this basis they go on to argue: "If the will is essentially and by its own nature indifferent to willing and not willing, it cannot determine itself to will; for that which determines anything must be determined, just as that which is determined must be indeterminate. But the will, when considered as determining itself, is both indeterminate and determined. Certainly our opponents do not postulate anything in the determining will which is not also present in the will being determined or already determinate, and, indeed, nothing can be postulated in it. Therefore, will cannot be determined by itself to will, but if not by itself then in some other manner." These are the very words of Professor Hereboord at Leiden.[13] He shows therein that by will he does not mean the mind but something else, either outside or inside the mind, rather like a *tabula rasa* lacking all thought and capable of receiving any picture whatsoever. Or perhaps like a weight in equilibrium, driven up or down according to the determination of any chance weight. Or

13 See his *Meletemata Philosophica*, 2nd edn. (Leiden, 1659).

perhaps it is something which neither he nor any mortal can grasp by thought. But we have just said, indeed, clearly shown, that the will is nothing but the mind itself, which we call a thinking thing, a thing which affirms and denies. Thus when we consider only the nature of the mind, we gather that the mind has an equal power of affirming and denying, for this, I claim, is to think. But if we infer the mind's power of affirming and denying from the fact that it thinks, why should we seek causes extrinsic to the mind to accomplish what follows solely from its nature? But, you say, the mind is not more determined to affirm than to deny, and so of necessity, you conclude, we must seek a cause to determine it. On the contrary, I reply that if the mind were essentially and by its own nature determined only to affirm (although to believe this is impossible as long as we think of mind as a thinking thing), then by its nature it could only affirm and never deny, no matter how many causes concurred in a denial. But if it were determined neither to affirm nor to deny, it could do neither. Finally, if it has the power to do both, it will be able to do either simply from its own nature and without the help of any other cause. This will be evident to everyone who regards a thinking thing as a thinking thing and does not separate the attribute of thought from the thinking thing, for the two are distinct only in reason. But our opponents do separate thought from thinking thing when they strip the thinking thing of its every thought and reduce it to something like the prime matter of the Peripatetics. Accordingly, I reply to their argument as follows, and especially to the major: If by will is meant a thing stripped of every thought, we grant that will is indeterminate in its own nature. But we deny that will is something stripped of thought. On the contrary, we claim that will is thought, that is, a power of affirming and denying, and by that certainly nothing else can be understood than a cause sufficing for both affirmation and denial. Besides, if will were indeterminate and deprived of every thought, we would also deny that any extrinsic cause could determine it except God through his infinite power of creation. For to think of a thinking thing without any thought is the same as thinking of an extended thing without extension.

13. *Why philosophers have confused mind with corporeal bodies.* Finally, so as not to rehearse a multitude of arguments here, I observe that our opponents have confused mind with corporeal bodies, because they have not understood will and possess no clear and distinct concept of mind. They were led to this because they used words ordinarily applied to corporeal things, to signify spiritual things which they did not understand. For they were accustomed to call bodies indeterminate when they are driven in opposite directions by equivalent, and contrary, external causes, and so remain in equilibrium. Thus, when they claim that will is indeterminate, they seem to think of it as a body placed in equilibrium; and since such bodies possess nothing but what they have received from external causes (from which it follows that they must always be determined by an external cause), they suppose that the same effect occurs in the will. But we have sufficiently explained how the matter actually stands, and so here we stop.

Of extended substance we have already said enough, and beyond these two we recognize no other substances. As for real accidents and other qualities, such concepts have been sufficiently exposed, so there is no need to waste time in refuting them. Here, then, we withdraw our hand from the page.

The Library of Liberal Arts